A Handbook
for Garden
Designers

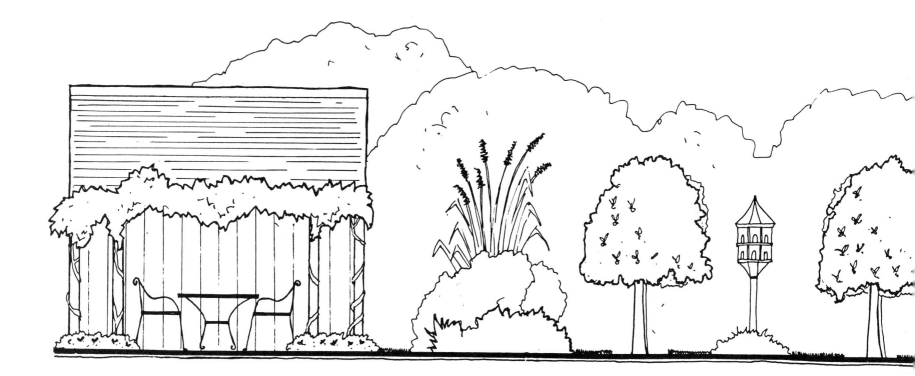

A Handbook for Garden Designers

ROSEMARY ALEXANDER FRSA
with Karena Batstone

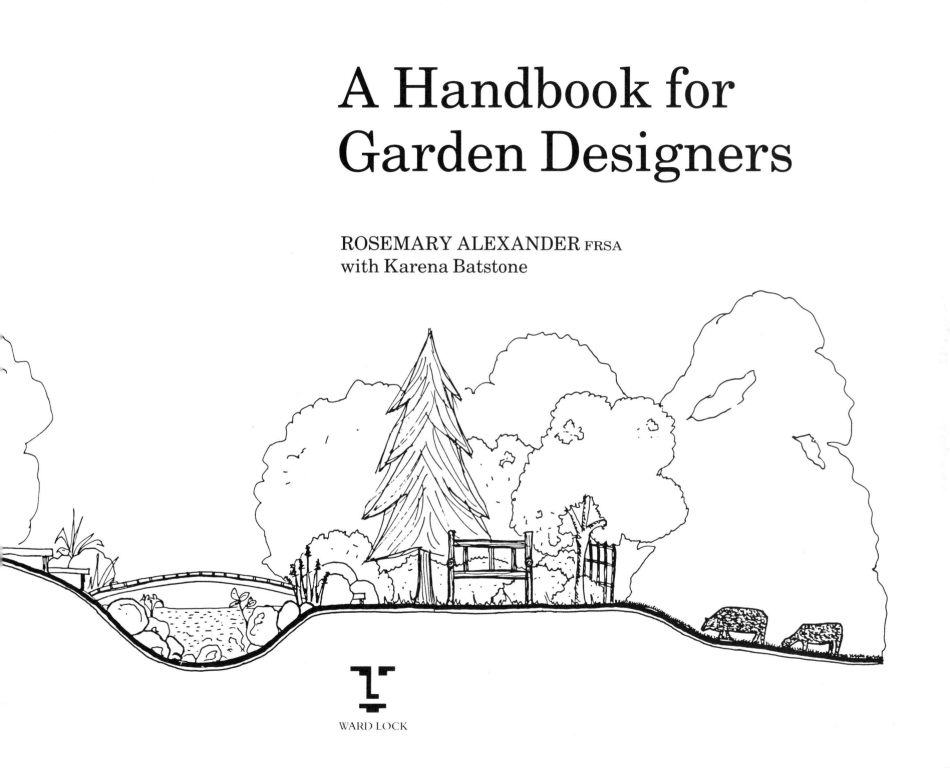

WARD LOCK

A WARD LOCK BOOK

First published in the UK 1994
by Ward Lock
Wellington House, 125 Strand
London WC2R 0BB

A Cassell Imprint

Reprinted 1994
First Paperback edition 1996
Reprinted 1998, 1999

Distributed in the United States
by Sterling Publishing Co. Inc.
387 Park Avenue South, New York, NY 10016-8810

A British Library Cataloguing in Publication Data block
for this book may be obtained from the British Library

ISBN 0 7063 7476 2

Typeset by Litho Link Ltd, Welshpool, Powys, Wales
Printed and bound in Great Britain by The Bath Press, Bath

Cover photograph: Derrick Witty

Contents

Acknowledgments 6

Preface................................7

Introduction 9

1 Necessary equipment.................. 10

2 Preliminary arrangements 24

3 The site survey 26

4 Drawing up the site plan 44

5 The site inventory and site analysis.........48

6 Developing the design 52

7 Presentation of plans.................. 62

8 The garden layout plan 66

9 Sections and elevations............. 72

10 The planting plan 82

11 Enhancing with visuals........... 96

12 Reproducing and presenting work...126

13 Establishing your own practice 132

Index...............................134

Acknowledgments

The authors would like to thank all who have helped in compiling this book, in particular the staff, tutors and students at the English Gardening School, especially Diana Abbott for typing and retyping the text. We also thank those who have allowed us to design their gardens – the plans for many of which appear here, and the following, whose work has been used in this book:

Georgina Bryson (pp. 63, 77, 103); Elizabeth Cochrane (p. 101); Hallie Cohn (p. 95); Zal Davar (p. 64); Anthony du Gard Pasley (p. 104); Ayuko Inoue (p. 119); IPC Magazines Ltd/Robert Harding Syndication/National Trust (p. 104); Sarah Janson (p. 63); Fred Jennett (pp. 17, 18); John Keyes, Keyes Landscape and Graham Rose (p. 21); Pamela Lane-Smith (pp. 75, 80, 102); Gwyn Lewis (p. 109); Candace Long Brewer (pp. 64, 97, 109); Helen Miller (pp. 78, 94); Geoff Moring (p. 64); Tara Owens (p. 79); Partridge Office Equipment (p. 13); Graham Slocombe, Landscape Software (p. 20, 22, 23); Ann Springford (p. 63); Helen Tindale (p. 98), Susanna Yeatman Biggs (p. 120).

Preface

In writing this book, we have tried to explain the surveying, draughting and planning techniques that we use as garden designers, and that we teach at the English Gardening School in London. No two designers will work in exactly the same way, and the intention of this book is to show what should be done, and how to do it, although we anticipate that most readers will adapt our suggestions to their own needs and environment.

In the past, garden plans were drawn individually for each client or garden, the work being executed in ink by skilled draughtsmen on cartridge paper as copying machines were not available. Today original work can be easily reproduced and all work, including the design process, must be carried out quickly and efficiently, as time spent on a project by the desiger will be reflected in the client's bill.

We have tried to show that, as in most professions, there are certain aids, such as the grid, which can help inspire the most inhibited designer. We have tried to show simple and speedy drawing techniques, and as we expect most of our readers to draw their own plans, we do not attempt to compete with the graphics of design consultants who may employ specialists to execute their beautiful and often complex plans.

After understanding and experimenting with your own drawings, we hope you will become more critical and analytical of the work of other designers, often adapting a particular technique to your own style. We hope you enjoy your work, and that we may help you to express your intentions clearly to persuade your clients to build beautiful gardens.

Rosemary Alexander

Karena Batstone

Introduction

Garden design is not simply a matter of choosing plants and arranging them on site. It is the culmination of a process that begins with the soil and the seasons and that involves everything from the construction of the garden to the way in which the client will use the space.

Although garden design is now a recognized profession, many of the most admired gardens, such as Sissinghurst in England, were laid out not by garden designers but by the owners of the properties themselves. Other gardens have evolved gradually, consecutive owners making alterations according to their needs or tastes. Frequently, fashion plays a part in these changes, people being influenced by magazines, television and other media. The increasing number of people visiting gardens over recent years has led to a greater interest in gardening and in garden design, with people trying to create in their own gardens what they have admired elsewhere. In Britain, many private gardens are open to the public, allowing other people to see what has been done and to ask how and why.

Home owners are now aware that a garden that is well laid out and well planted is an asset to be enjoyed and exploited, rather than a luxury to be considered if time and resources allow. These home owners may have admired the gardens of their friends and neighbours, but they are often themselves inexperienced in horticulture or too busy to design and plant their own gardens.

Garden centres can offer the materials, tools and plants, but the staff, even if they are qualified to do so, can rarely spare the time to visit the site and advise on garden layout. Home owners who want to redesign their gardens would save both time and money by calling in a garden designer, who will plan the space according to a client's requirements and the limitations of the site. Garden designers are often also used by house or hotel developers and by interior designers, who realize that their specialist expertise can greatly enhance a property.

Normally a garden designer will be responsible not only for designing the garden but also for suggesting a competent firm of builders to construct it. The designer will usually oversee the work, liaising with the owner about any alterations to the plan, supervising the planting and arranging for future maintenance. In some cases the clients may want only a planting plan or they may wish to construct the garden themselves, and most designers are accustomed to complying with the individual requirements of their clients. In many cases a designer will continue to advise a client as the garden develops.

1
Necessary equipment

In order to communicate ideas to a client the designer will usually survey the site and then draw up the survey to scale as the basis for a future design. Both surveying and draughting equipment will be necessary, and although a professional surveyor may sometimes be used, the designer will learn much more about the site by taking the survey personally.

Surveying equipment

You will need:

- **30m (100ft) tape measure**, preferably the modern, plasticized version, or two measures if the site is large (1).........................☐

- **metal skewer** secured with wire to the end of the tape (2) ....☐

- **damp cloth** for cleaning the tape ....☐

- **2m (6ft) or 10m (33ft) rigid spring tape or measuring rod** for taking short dimensions, such as the height of steps or low walls (3).......☐

- **double clip board** to keep out the wind or rain when making notes (4) ....☐

- **graph paper** to help keep the lines straight when taking measurements (5) ....☐

- **note book**, A4 ($11\frac{2}{3} \times 8\frac{1}{4}$in) (6) ....☐

- **pencils, eraser and pens** in a case (7)...☐

- **ball of smooth, thick string** for setting out lines that may be too long for the tape measure, plus garden canes (8)......................☐

- **spirit level, pegs and a wooden plank** if simple levelling is required (9) ....☐

- **camera**, spare film and batteries, and a tripod (optional) (10)..☐

- **compass** to ascertain the north (11) ....☐

- **existing plans**, maps and plans for any proposed house extension or conservatory if available (12)...☐

- **trowel and plastic bags and labels** for taking soil for pH testing (13)..........................☐

- **suitable clothing**, warm and waterproof if necessary..☐

- **bag** or holdall to keep all the equipment clean and dry ....☐

How to use the equipment

Tape measure Before you buy a tape measure, make sure that all measurements are clear and easy to read and that the tape itself is strong and winds in easily. At the end of the tape there is usually a metal ring or hook, which can be slipped over a cane, hooked on to something or held by an assistant. Make sure that you count this ring as part of the measurement, otherwise all your dimensions will be slightly out. Keep the tape clean by always winding it in between a piece of damp cloth so that any dirt or dust picked up from the site is removed. If this is not done the inside of the case can easily become clogged. If you are unfamiliar with using a tape measure, practise measuring simple heights and widths and noting them down. In this way you will become familiar with the figures and will be less likely to make mistakes when measuring a real site.

Metal skewer This should be about 150mm (6 in) long and should be fastened with wire or string to the ring or hook at the end of the tape. It can then be stuck into any convenient crack or into the soil or lawn and obviates the need for an assistant to hold the end of the tape measure.

Rigid spring tape This is particularly useful and quick for measuring vertical dimensions, such as steps or walls, where a long tape measure would be inconvenient. Again, take care to avoid getting dirt inside the casing.

Double clip board This is invaluable for protecting notes, graph paper or plans from wind or rain when you are on site, because the upper side can be used as a shield when you are writing notes. A tough, plasticized, wipe-clean material is preferable.

▶ Surveying equipment.

Graph paper Buy paper that has reasonably large and clear squares and subdivisions rather than feint-ruled paper, which is difficult to read. If the site is small it is quite possible to draw it to scale while you are surveying by marking each major square as 1, 2 or even 5 metres (yards) and using the subdivisions to write down the actual measurements. An A4 ($11\frac{2}{3} \times 8\frac{1}{4}$ in) or A3 ($16\frac{1}{2} \times 11\frac{2}{3}$ in) pad is recommended.

Notebook Ideally, this should have lined paper and be fairly sturdy.

Pencils, eraser and pens in plastic case An assortment of these, in good working order, is useful because different colours can be used to denote different things, making the survey notes easier to read and transcribe.

Ball of smooth string In larger gardens some dimensions may be too long to take with a tape measure. If you set up a dimension line with string and garden canes you can take the measurements by running the tape measure along the string and marking each 30 metres (yards) or so off on it. You will find this is particularly useful when you are triangulating across a large site.

Spirit level, pegs and wooden plank These are useful for gauging minor changes in level, such as a gentle slope across a garden. By setting up the pegs, balancing the plank on them and then checking with a spirit level, slight changes can be assessed without using expensive surveying equipment. Surveying equipment, such as a dumpy level or a theodolite, can be hired if necessary.

Camera, spare film and batteries Almost any camera will suffice, but an adjustable, wide angle/standard lens is particularly useful. Film must be suited to the climatic conditions, to what is being photographed and to the purpose for which the photographs are to be used. A tripod is useful for producing more professional photographs.

Existing plans If they are available these can save hours of measuring and drawing. Architects' plans can be reduced or enlarged as necessary and are very accurate. Maps drawn to scales of 1 : 1250 or 1 : 12500 are too small to be accurate when enlarged, although they can be used as the basis for a more accurate survey.

Compass You will need to be able to ascertain the north, which will, in turn, determine sunny and shady areas within the garden.

Trowel, plastic bags and labels You will need to take soil samples to be tested for their pH levels. Each sample should be clearly labelled, to indicate from exactly where it was taken.

Warm and waterproof clothing Although this may seem obvious, waterproof clothing is often overlooked. Surveying can be a cold, lengthy operation, and it will seem more so if you are unsuitably dressed.

Drawing equipment

You will need:

- **drawing board**, A1 ($33\frac{1}{8} \times 23\frac{1}{2}$in) or A2 ($23\frac{1}{2} \times 16\frac{1}{2}$in) size, with parallel motion (1) ...☐

- **T-square** if parallel motion is not available (2) ....☐

- **tracing paper**, A1 ($33\frac{1}{8} \times 23\frac{1}{2}$in) or A2 ($23\frac{1}{2} \times 16\frac{1}{2}$in) size and smaller.....................☐

- **graph paper**, A1 ($33\frac{1}{8} \times 23\frac{1}{2}$in) or A2 ($23\frac{1}{2} \times 16\frac{1}{2}$in) size and smaller.....................☐

- **technical drawing pens** of nib sizes 0.7, 0.5, 0.35 and 0.25 plus black specialist ink (3) ....☐

- **felt-tip pens or drawing markers** ....☐

- **graphite pencils** with HB and B leads, or clutch pencil and leads, or 0.5mm constant-width pencils (4) ....☐

- **pencil sharpener** (5) ....☐

- **eraser** for ink and pencil (6).......................☐

- **erasing shield** for precision erasing (7) ......☐

- **scalpel and razor blades** for scratching out (8) ....☐

- **set-square** (9)...☐

- **masking tape** (10) ....☐

- **protractor** for simple angles (11) ....☐

- **adjustable set-square** with angle scale (12) ....☐

- **compasses** with extension arm and ink attachment (13)...☐

- **metric scale** to include 1 : 1, 1 : 50, 1 : 100, 1 : 200, 1 : 1250, 1 : 2500 (14)............☐

▶ Draughting equipment.

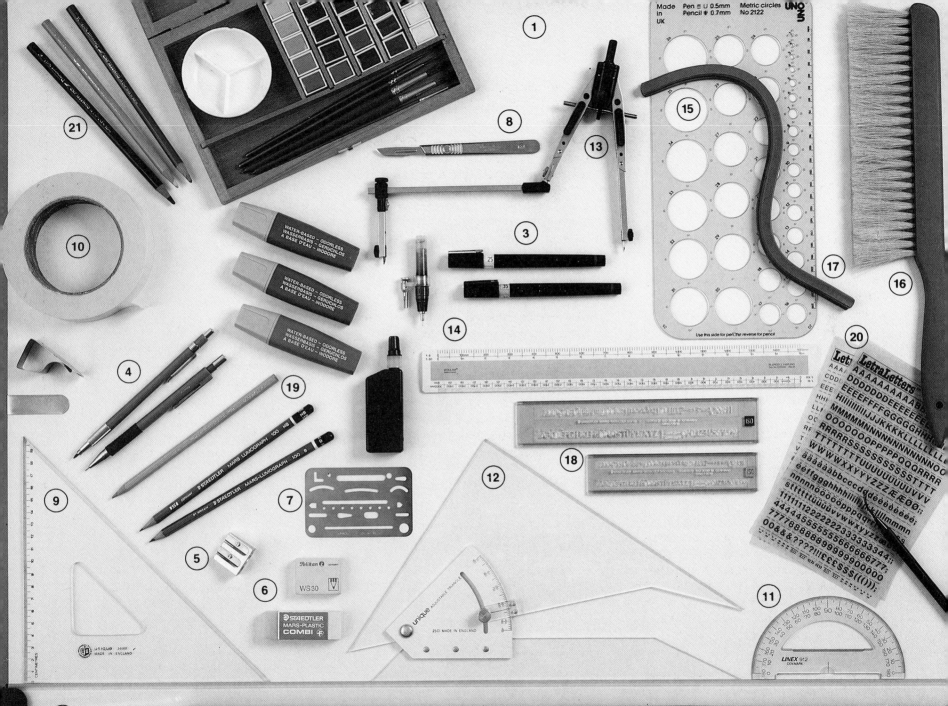

- **circle template** with bevelled edges for ink work (15) .... ☐
- **drawing board brush or duster** (16) .... ☐
- **flexi-curve**, at least 300mm (12in) long (17) .. ☐
- **plastic tube** for carrying drawings .... ☐

For lettering and colouring up:

- **lettering stencils** to fit pen sizes (18) .... ☐
- **non-photo pencil** (i.e., one that is not reproduced on a print) (19) .... ☐
- **dry-transfer lettering sheets** (20) .... ☐
- **coloured pencils or watercolours** for colouring up plans (21) .... ☐

How to use the equipment

Drawing board Drawing boards are made to correspond with the standard drawing paper sizes. The board can be as basic or as sophisticated as you like. The most basic is simply a flat piece of board. The more advanced are laminated boards with parallel motion (a sliding horizontal ruler), which can be either table mounted or free standing. The basic board is perfectly suitable for the beginner, but all types of drawing board should have faces that are perfectly flat and smooth, so that they will not twist or buckle with normal use. Edges should be at right-angles to one another. Do not stick drawing pins into your board or use it for cutting because you may harm the surface. It is easier to draw accurately on an angled surface, so if you buy a basic board, use a block of wood or a telephone directory to raise the edge furthest away from you, thus angling the board towards you. You may need to try several different heights before you find the most comfortable angle.

T-square So-named from their shape, T-squares are required for the basic board if you do not have a parallel motion board. The T-square is used for all horizontal line drawing, the head of the T-square being held against the left-hand side of the board. Try to find one made of clear perspex. Do not use your T-square as a cutting edge or you will damage it.

Tracing paper It is useful to have several sizes, although if you buy A1 (33⅛ × 23½in) sheets you can always cut them down. They can be bought in pads or in single sheets and in various weights – for example, 60gsm, 90gsm and 120gsm – or in rolls. You will throw a lot of tracing paper away while you are working up a design, and so it is advisable to use the lightest, 60gsm, until your design is finalized – the lighter the weight, the cheaper the paper. You can then do your final drawing on a slightly heavier weight.

Until you know the size you are most likely to use – you are unlikely to use A1 (33⅛ × 23½in) unless you are doing a design for a large garden – buy the paper in sheets of A2 (23½ × 16½in). You can always buy an A4 (11⅔ × 8¼in) pad for small sketches.

Paper You can buy this as you go along but in the first instance you will need one or two sheets of A1 (33⅛ × 23½in) metric graph paper. You will not draw on this, but it will be the first sheet of paper to be put on your board and will serve as your backing sheet.

Technical drawing pens These are required for drawing with ink on tracing paper, but do not use them on ordinary paper because the nibs will become clogged. The pens are expensive to buy, and you will have to practise to get even lines. The nibs come in a variety of sizes, which correspond to the thickness of line – 0.25, 0.35, 0.5 and 0.7 are the most useful – and extra nibs can be bought. The pens must be properly looked after so that they do not become clogged with ink. They should be held upright against the T-square or set-square so that the ink flows evenly. Use a smooth, even pressure to draw all lines. An alternative to technical pens are the disposable drawing pens that are now available.

Protractor Use a protractor to measure or set out angles. It should be placed so that the centre coincides with the apex of the angle.

Set-square This triangle of, usually, clear plastic is used for vertical and diagonal line drawing when rested on the edge of the T-square. Get the largest size you can or you will have trouble drawing long vertical lines. The length of the longest side should be around 250–300mm (10–12in). If you intend to do your final drawing in ink, make sure you buy a set-square that has angled edges, which help to eliminate smudging. You will need both a 45° angle set-square and an

Standard drawing paper sizes.

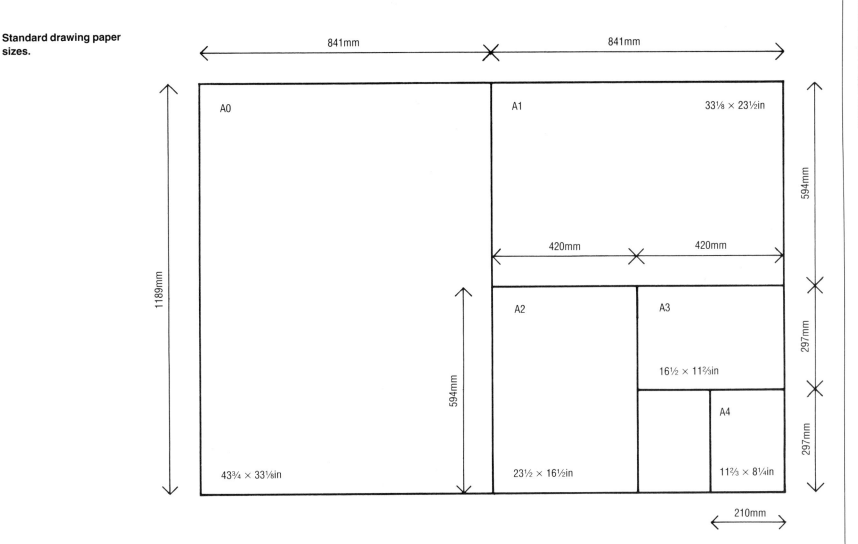

adjustable set-square to carry out axonometric and other drawing.

Compasses You will need a pair of compasses for drawing up your survey and for larger circles and curves. Purchase a pair with an extension arm for doing the survey and for making large circles, plus an ink attachment for working up final drawings.

Pencils and pens It is useful to have a selection of pencils with graphite leads varying in degrees of hardness and softness, although you will usually need HB and B. The cost of the pencil will be proportionate to its usefulness. Cheap pencils have gritty, crumbly leads, which smudge. Hard lead tends to eat into the surface of the paper. The most useful grades are H (hard), used for technical drawing, HB and 2B (soft), used for

freehand drawing and 3B, which is used for shading. An alternative to the ordinary pencil is the fine-lead pencil, a form of 'clutch' pencil, which does not require sharpening as the diameter of the lead represents the point size. A 0.5mm diameter is the easiest to use. Other types of clutch pencil are also available, but these require an appropriate sharpener to keep the point sharp.

Coloured pencils/water soluble pencils There are some excellent brands, but the colours need to be carefully chosen so that they are appropriate for garden design – use natural shades and pastels, rather than bright or harsh colours.

Scales Scales are narrow strips of plastic the length of a normal ruler and either flat or triangular in shape. They have varying numbers of divisions along each edge on both sides. The divisions are in proportion to actual distances and dimensions and are used for making plans drawn to scale. The scales most often used are 1 : 50, and 1 : 100, but most scales go up to at least 1 : 1250 or 1: 2500. If you wish to work in imperial scale the nearest equivalent to 1 : 50 and 1 : 100 is ¼in : 12in and ⅛in : 12 in. The use of a scale rule is much easier in practice than it is in theory.

Pencil sharpeners If you to draw accurately it is most important that you sharpen pencil leads frequently. Any type of pencil sharpener can be used, but often an ordinary pen knife and sandpaper produce the best results. The point can be rounded with the sandpaper so that it does not cut into the paper and so that it wears away evenly and remains a constant distance from any straight edge.

Eraser This should be a combination of soft rubber for erasing pencil work and a special composition rubber, which removes ink without damaging the surface of the paper. The accumulated small particles of rubber should be brushed or dusted off the paper.

Erasing shield This thin piece of metal is laid over the drawing to mask anything that is not intended for erasure.

Drawing board brush or duster You will need a simple soft brush or duster to keep drawings clean by removing graphite dust or eraser shavings from them. Sweep your drawings regularly as you work on them.

Circle template This useful device has 20 or 30 different sized circles for drawing small circles, such as pots or avenues of trees. Make sure that the largest circle is about 50mm (2in) in diameter. A bevelled edge is useful to prevent ink smudges, and if several circles of the same size are to be drawn, it is helpful to mark this circle with a small piece of masking tape so that the wrong size is not used in error.

Flexi-curve A hollow strip of plastic filled with a bendable metal strip is useful as a guide for drawing curves. The pen or pencil must be carefully rested upon the flexible shape and smooth, even pressure applied.

Plastic tube When you transport drawings to the printers or to clients you will need to protect them.

Non-photo pencil Use these pencils to draw guidelines on plans. These lines will not print and will not, therefore, need to be erased.

Scalpel and razor blades Although you will use your eraser to remove most mistakes or revisions, a scalpel and blades will probably also be necessary. The blade should be curved, not pointed, as it is much easier to use and will do less harm to the surface of the paper. Remember to rub the damaged paper surface with an eraser to restore it, otherwise the technical pen ink will 'bleed' or the lines will appear too thick.

For lettering or colouring

Stencils Lettering templates or stencils will act as a guide for pens. A variety of sloping and upright styles are available, and, although practice is needed in using them, stencils are very useful if you want to make certain headings stand out. They are also useful when several people work on a drawing but the handwriting must remain uniform.

Dry-transfer lettering sheets These thin, plastic sheets, on which a variety of letters, numerals and punctuation marks are printed, are also known as pressure-transfer lettering sheets. The characters are applied by rubbing them over with moderate pressure with a pen, knife or similar burnisher. The silicone-treated backing sheets not only prevent sheets from sticking to each other but, by being laid over the letters and then burnished, can help their adhesion. These letters can also be sprayed with a fixative to keep them in place. Dry-transfer lettering sheets are expensive and should be stored flat, away from excessive heat or humidity. Keep a catalogue of the available pressure transfers in your office for quick reference.

Coloured pencils and watercolours There are so many of these to choose from that it is wise to experiment until you find a medium that suits your style and capability. Whether you use simple children's crayons in basic colours or pastels or watercolour, the application of colour to a drawing can enliven the effect and make the drawing easier to understand.

Lettering and titling on drawings

Almost every drawing will require the addition of some descriptive words or notes to clarify the meaning, but if the lettering lacks confidence, it can seriously undermine what may otherwise be an effective drawing. It is worthwhile developing a particular style, which will then be used on all your work.

The garden designer ought to be proficient in three different types of lettering, as a combination of the three will be used on most plans and title blocks. These are freehand lettering, stencil or guided-pen lettering and dry-transfer lettering.

For speed and consistency most notes on a drawing should be written freehand, in either pencil or pen depending on the medium that has been used for the drawing. Stencils or guided-pen lettering may be used for headings and titles, and dry-transfer lettering can be added to make certain points stand out. Whatever you decide to use, you should aim to achieve:

- consistency
- legibility
- style
- spacing
- speed

Strive for consistent letter forms, consistent spacing between letters and words, consistent style and a consistent line weight.

The legibility of your work will depend on the shape and form of each letter, the spacing between the letters, the way in which the words are arranged and the variation of the sizes and positions of lettering according to their importance. An overexaggerated style can be as difficult to read as an underexaggerated one.

Copy and experiment and choose what is comfortable for you. Do not exaggerate or get too stylistic. Remember to keep the lettering legible and bear in mind that acceptable styles are vertical or slanted forwards, vertical being more commonly used.

Aim for close spacing between letters in words and wider spacing between words. Spacing between lines of lettering will depend on how much space is available, but spacing can be fairly close, with more space left between paragraphs. The longer the line, the greater the spacing between those lines should be.

It is necessary to develop a style that can be executed quickly, while still remaining consistent and legible. Freehand writing is always quicker than stencil or dry-transfer lettering.

Before you experiment with lettering, examine your own natural style. Is it upright or sloping? Try to adapt your natural style to the freehand writing that you will use on plans. The stencil or dry-transfer lettering can be in the same style, or it can be a complete contrast, which may relieve monotony on a drawing, making the notes easier to read. The size of the letters should be based on the importance of the notes on the drawing.

▼ **This style of lettering is quick to draw and easy to read.**

ABCDEFGHIJKLMNOPQRSTUVWXYZ

abcdefghijklmnopqrstuvwxyz

1234567890

TO AID LEGIBILITY AVOID

VARYING THE LETTER HEIGHT

THE LETTER SPACING

THE LETTER WEIGHT

THE LETTER SLANT

For presentation work, it is helpful to place a fresh sheet of tracing paper over the drawn plan, mapping out the notes around the different elements to strengthen the overall composition. It is better to organize the notes in blocks rather than to splatter them over the entire sheet. When you have decided exactly what you want to say and where it will be located, this tracing paper overlay can be placed under the plan, to act as a guide for the final lettering.

Freehand lettering guidelines

To achieve clear, consistent lettering, always use guidelines. These are thin, horizontal lines drawn lightly, either in pencil on the final sheet, to be erased later, or on a sheet that is placed under the final drawing. If a non-photo pencil is used to draw the guidelines directly on to the final sheet, it will not reproduce when copied. The guidelines will help you to maintain consistent letter dimensions and spacings.

To draw the guidelines begin by drawing the upper and lower lines, and then add the third line halfway between them. All crossbars should connect along this third line.

On most plans, irrespective of whether the lettering is completed in freehand or by stencil or dry-transfer, only three or four sizes of letter are required. The actual size of the letters ought to be in proportion to the size of the sheet and to the type of drawing. Normally these three or four sizes will be used on most plans, so it may be worth taking time to draw up rows of the guidelines in a fine ink line so that they can remain as an office 'tool' and be used as a guide behind all drawings.

Another short cut to lettering guides is to collect sheets of lined paper of varying dimensions, which can be slipped behind the final sheet, secured with masking tape and used as a backing for lettering. Even the actual gridded graph paper backing sheet can be used as a guide, but the 'three-line' guideline usually produces the best result. Always practise for a while before beginning the actual presentation lettering.

Lining up lettering For consistency and clarity, all lettering should be lined up to a margin or margins. This will ensure that the first letter of each new line follows exactly beneath the first letter of the preceding line. A similar margin, or end point, should occur at the opposite side, the effect being similar to that achieved on a typewriter or word processor. Again, these margin lines can be drawn in with a non-photo pencil.

FOR EASY READING ALWAYS USE INVISIBLE MARGINS TO ORGANISE YOUR TEXT INTO BLOCKS OF EQUAL WIDTH

WITHOUT THEM THE EYE IS LED ALL OVER THE PLACE AND THE READER IS DISTRACTED FROM THE MESSAGE OF THE TEXT

▲ **Invisible margins should be used to align the first letter of each line.**

Underlining Underlining certain lettering may help it to stand out, and when you draw any line, the emphasis should always be on the end-points of each line, avoiding the tendency to decrease pressure at the end of the stroke.

Pencil weight Keep the weights of pencil lines consistent and use an HB lead because an H lead will tend to bite into the paper and a B lead will tend to smudge. A small sheet of tracing paper can be used under your hand to prevent smudging. Always begin at the top of a sheet and work down, keeping the pencil weight consistent and sharpening the lead when necessary. After sharpening, the pencil lead may need to be worked or slightly blunted before it will look consistent with the work just executed.

In general, the verticals of letters should be drawn with a thin line, while the horizontals can be drawn boldly with thicker lines. The technique of using a small set-square to draw all vertical lines can also be effective but needs to be practised before it can be done quickly.

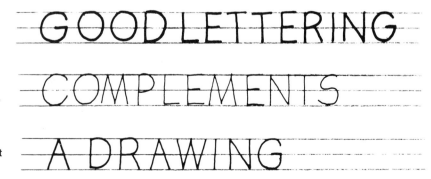

▶ **Guidelines will help to keep your lettering even in size and shape. The spacing between each line of words must also be consistent.**

GOOD LETTERING COMPLEMENTS A DRAWING

Stencilling or guided-pen lettering

Stencils can be used for titling drawings or notes and, when they are used properly, they will produce a clear, uniform result. They can be made of metal but are more usually clear plastic, sometimes with a fine metal supporting strip at both top and bottom. Stencils are available in a wide range of lettering styles and sizes, but make sure that the chosen size will accommodate your nib size. Stencils are made in sizes to correspond with the nib size of technical ink pens, and if the nib size is large, it will not fit into the letters; if it is smaller, the nib will move about and produce uneven lettering. The stencil plate must be held firmly down with one hand against your parallel motion or T-square, while the other hand is used to hold the pen. The parallel motion or T-square must be held firmly, and the stencil moved backwards and forwards against it until the line is completed. The pen must be held in an upright position so that the ink flows freely. Spacing between letters must be done by eye, with closer spacing between letters and wider spacing between words.

At first, stencils may appear difficult to use, but with practice they can be quick and effective, and are very useful in producing uniformity in lettering when several people are working on a drawing, although similar spacing must be followed. The stencils should be kept clean and washed occasionally to prevent ink clogging the letters.

123456...
STENCIL LETTERING IS CLEAR AND UNIFORM

▲ **Stencil lettering is easy to read and produces a uniform result.**

Dry-transfer lettering

This type of lettering tends to be rather expensive, so it should be used with discretion. Many different styles of lettering are available, printed on thin plastic sheets, which also include numbers and punctuation. Sheets including compass points and other symbols are also available. Each sheet is supplied with and is protected by a silicone backing sheet, which doubles as a burnishing sheet and should on no account be thrown away.

To apply the letters or symbols to a drawing, remove the backing sheet and place the letters appropriately on the drawing. Use the guidelines on the sheets to ensure that the letters are straight and evenly spaced. Shade across each character with a burnisher, ball-point pen or similiar, moving from top to bottom with moderate pressure. Continue until the letter appears lighter, which means that it has been detached from the sheet and has adhered to the surface of the paper. Peel back the film carefully, and reposition it to transfer the next letter. After completing each word, or a few letters, lay over the backing sheet and burnish with a blunt instrument to make sure that the letters are firmly stuck down, otherwise they may begin to peel off when the drawing is being copied. A matt fixative spray can also be used to make sure that all the letters adhere to the drawing, but mask all other areas to protect them against the spray. Accidental application of letters can be removed by scratching with a razor blade or scalpel or lifting with draughting tape, and incomplete letters can be made up by using a combination of others or by touching up with Indian ink.

Position the first letter and rub it down firmly with a burnisher. Lightly rub down some of the space marks below to use as a guide.

Use the space marks to align each letter before rubbing down.

After removing the space marks with masking tape or a scalpel, the letters should be fixed down by burnishing through the backing sheet.

▲ **Use this technique to apply dry-transfer lettering.**

The use of computers

Although a computer is by no means an essential piece of equipment at any stage of the garden design process, this book would be incomplete without a reference to some of the areas in which you may find computer systems useful. One would be hard pressed these days to find a business that does not depend on computer systems for some aspects of its operation, and the garden design business is no exception.

In recent years, following the increased use of computer aided design (CAD) by architects and surveyors, several programs have been developed that are specifically aimed at the landscape/garden designer. CAD programs exist to help designers draw plans and visuals quickly, although if you are used to drawing with conventional equipment, you may find that your ideas are inhibited when you are faced with a graphics tablet and a light pen. The initial cost of a suitable CAD system is often beyond the bounds of most small practices, and it does take time to acquire the necessary computing skills, but new, more user-friendly systems are appearing regularly and the costs, particularly of the hardware, are coming down all the time.

More useful to many designers are the specialist plant databases that exist to help you save time in selecting plants for your planting plan. These provide an encyclopedia of the most commonly used plants in cultivation, with details, for each, on a large number of topics, such as country of origin, leaf colour, site aspect, design use and plant form. The advantage of such a database over the plant lists available in books is that the computer system can be indexed in many ways. A plant database enables you to search quickly for plants to meet any number of given requirements – for instance, you can ask it to give you a list of all the plants that will thrive in a sandy soil, flower in June and have fragrant flowers. With some programs you can add more plants to the list and alter any existing plant attributes.

Apart from plant databases there are also programs available for the garden designer to assist in general office management. Some programs can help you to produce plant schedules, bills of quantity and costings. The costing variables are usually set up for a typical landscape design business, but they can be tailored to your own requirements. There are also programs that include time logs, for project monitoring purposes, address databases, to keep track of your suppliers, clients and so on, and word processor files.

Simple word processors are relatively inexpensive and have many uses for the garden designer. Much word processor software gives the user the option of choosing from several fonts, or typefaces, which can enhance the appearance of your plans and provide a professional looking finish. If they are used to produce sections of text or even individual labels, you would simply print out the text onto tracing paper or computer paper, depending on what kind of paper your printer accepts, and stick it down on your plan. When you reproduce the plan, however, you would have to use the photocopying method, as the dyeline process would reveal the added strips of paper.

PLANT DATABASE & INDEX

BROADLEAF TREES	F2	GRASS	F4A
BROADLEAF SHRUBS	F3	MATRIX PLANTING	F5A
CLIMBERS	F4	TOP & SOFT FRUIT	F6A
CONIFEROUS TREES	F5	INTERIOR PLANTS	F9S
CONIFEROUS SHRUBS	F6	ANNUALS	F2C
HERBACEOUS	F7	ALL PLANTS	F1C
ALPINES	F8	PROJECT TOTALS	F7A
BULBS	F8A	PLANT PRICE INDEX	F3C
AQUATICS	F2A	PLANTING CHARGE INDEX	F3S
HT-ROSES	F3A	BOT.NAME/SERIAL No.INDEX	F4S
ASSOCIATIONS FILE 1 (Woodland, Wild & Cottage Themes)			F4C
ASSOCIATIONS FILE 2 (Meadow, Sub-Tropical & Modern Themes)			F5C
GENERAL FILES INDEX	F7C	EXIT TO DOS	F6C
HELP	F1	RETURN TO MAIN MENU	F10

◄ **This plant database is divided into several sections, allowing quick access to any specific plant. It can also be used as one complete encyclopedia.**

▼ An example of a trellis design produced using a CAD program.

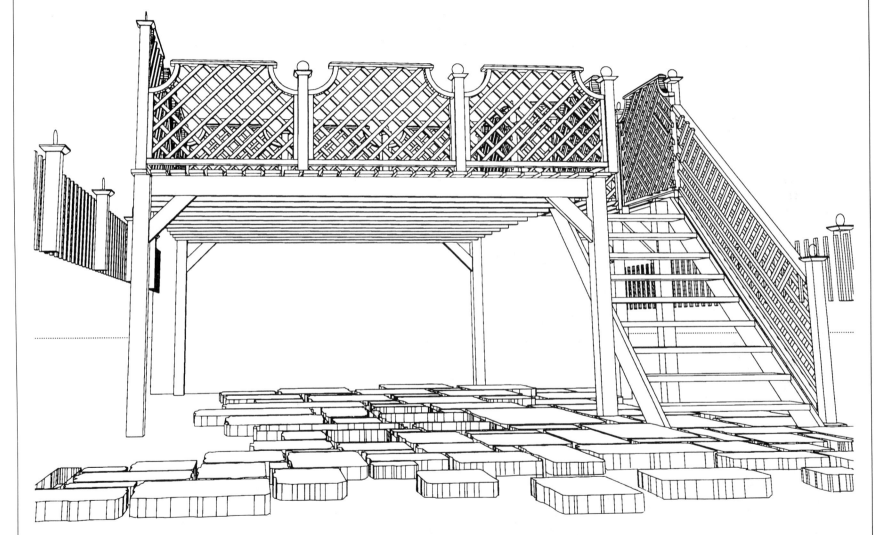

▼ Printouts from a range of computer programs aimed at assisting the garden designer.

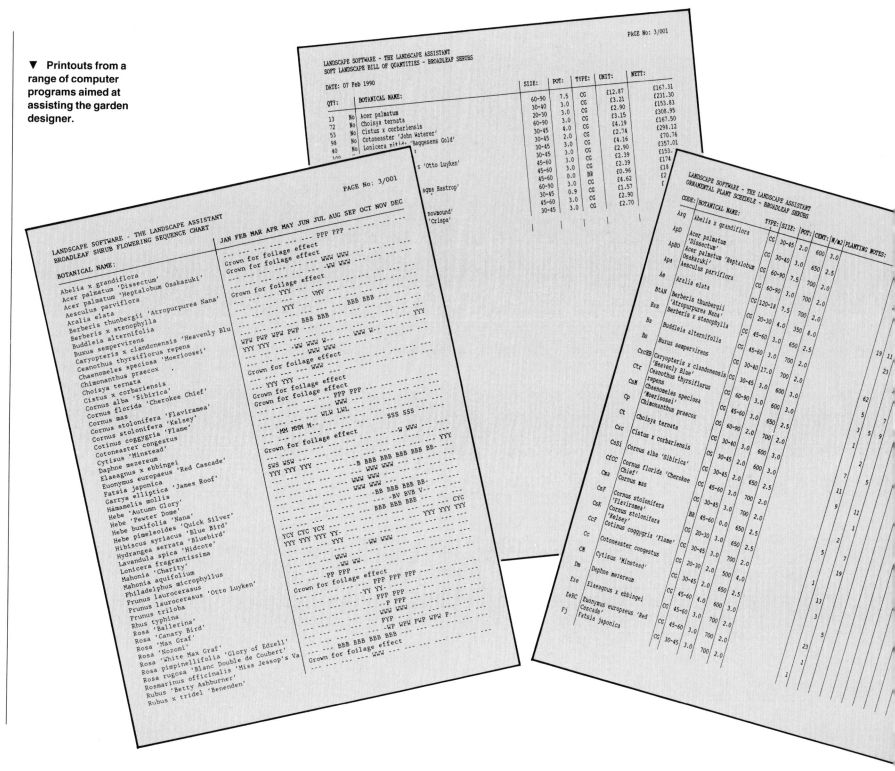

LANDSCAPE SOFTWARE - THE LANDSCAPE ASSISTANT
PLANT INFORMATION SHEET - BROADLEAF SHRUBS

BOTANICAL NAME:	Lavandula spica 'Hidcote'
COMMON NAME:	Lavander
PHONETIC SPELLING:	Lav-and-u-la spi-ka Hid-cote
FAMILY NAME:	Labiatae
ORIGIN:	Hybrid
SIZE:	Dwarf Small
PLANT TYPE:	Hardy Evergreen Exotic
GROWTH RATE:	Fast
SEASON:	All year July August September
FLOWER COLOUR:	Blue
LEAF COLOUR:	Mid Green Grey
FRUIT COLOUR:	Not grown for fruit effect
BARK / STEM COLOUR:	Not grown for bark effect
TEXTURE:	Fine
FORM:	Rounded
DESIGN FUNCTION:	Group Groundcover Hedge(informal)
SPECIAL ATTRIBUTES:	Fragrant Wildlife
TOLERANCE:	Maritime
ASPECT:	Sun
SOIL DRAINAGE:	Well Drained Dry
CODE:	LsH
PRUNING:	Clip after flowering
SUSCEPTIBILITY:	None
PROPOGATION:	Cuttings
ROOT SYSTEM:	No available information
NOTES:	

LANDSCAPE SOFTWARE - THE LANDSCAPE ASSISTANT
SUPPLY & PLANT BUDGET ESTIMATE:

PAGE No: 0/001

Date: 07 Feb 1990
NB: Valid for six months from the above date

ITEM:	DESCRIPTION OF ITEMS:
01	Earthworks & Ground Modelling
02	Cultivation & Fertiliser Application
03	Weed Clearance & Herbicide Application
04	Broadleaf Tree Planting
05	Broadleaf Shrub Planting
06	Coniferous Tree Planting
07	Coniferous Shrub Planting
08	Climber Planting
09	Herbaceous Planting
10	Alpine Planting
12	Bulb Planting
11	Aquatic Planting
13	Hybrid Tea Rose Planting
14	Top & Soft Fruit Planting
15	Indoor Planting
16	Annual Planting
17	Matrix "A" Planting
18	Matrix "B" Planting
19	Matrix "C" Planting
20	Matrix "D" Planting
21	Grass Seeding
22	Turf Laying
23	Mulching
24	Maintenance

TOTALS:

NETT:

VAT:

GROSS:

LANDSCAPE SOFTWARE - THE LANDSCAPE ASSISTANT
PROJECT MONITORING ANALYSIS JOB No: 1039
CLIENT   : Dennis Chick
PROJECT TITLE: Garden Design
DATE   : 11 Feb 1990

PAGE No: 001

DATE:	DETAILS:	COST : NETT :	CHARGE OUT: NETT:	VAT:	GROSS:	MARGIN:
07-02-90	Concept design plan	£250.00	£287.50	£43.13	£330.63	£37.50
07-02-90	Printing Concept design plan	£5.50	£6.33	£0.95	£7.28	£0.83
23-03-90	Planting plan production	£132.00	£151.80	£22.77	£174.57	£19.80
27-04-90	Schedules	£2.45	£2.82	£0.42	£3.24	£0.37
27-04-90	Miscellaneous	£11.20	£12.88	£1.93	£14.81	£1.68
17-01-90	Site visit for survey	£48.00	£55.20	£8.28	£63.48	£7.20
07-02-90	Drawing sheets	£5.57	£6.41	£0.96	£7.37	£0.84
07-02-90	Creating plant schedules.	£9.25	£10.64	£1.60	£12.24	£1.39
07-02-90	Planting plans 301, 302, 303.	£8.40	£9.66	£1.45	£11.11	£1.26
Totals:		£472.37	£543.24	£81.49	£624.73	£70.87

2
Preliminary arrangements

The initial enquiry from a possible client may be made by telephone, by letter or even through casual conversation over dinner. Too often, however, the client who wishes to have a garden redesigned does not realize what is involved, assuming that it is merely a question of obtaining a few plants and popping them in! Most designers are either properly trained, or have years of experience behind them – often both. They will, therefore, expect to be paid for passing on their expertise, and will work for a set hourly rate in the same way as any other professional, be it doctor, dentist or design consultant.

Client enquiries and scale of fees

The services that you as a garden designer can offer and can expect to be paid for should be clearly established at the earliest stage so that no misunderstanding can occur. Travelling time, petrol and incidental expenses such as camera film and prints of drawings will also need to be charged to the client. The simplest way of doing this is to write down in logical order all that you are able to do for your client – from surveying to finding a contractor to build the garden or to finish off the planting.

Naturally, your client will want to know how much you will charge for doing all this. This is called a scale of fees and it is either typed as a letter or, more usually, presented as a printed card, with the name, adddress and telephone number of the designer, and frequently an identifying logo (see page 132).

On receiving an enquiry, the scale of fees should be sent to the client or garden owner well in advance of a first meeting to set out the method of working. A telephone call, ostensibly to check the time and date of the meeting, can also ascertain whether the garden owner has received the scale of fees and whether or not it is acceptable. Some designers charge for the first visit or consultation; others do not, taking a gamble on being offered the work. However, it is vital at the initial meeting to establish a good working relationship, the garden owner respecting the knowledge and reputation of the designer, and similarly the designer respecting and interpreting the wishes of the client. The client may even be familiar with the work of the designer, having specially chosen him or her to create a certain style of garden.

Visiting the site

Even if you are uncertain if you will be offered the job of redesigning the garden, it is sensible to be well prepared for this first meeting, even to the extent of adding an extra half-hour to the journey time to see other gardens in the neighbourhood. This will give you an idea of what will or will not grow and will also therefore indicate soil type, climate and so on. The site may be small and the clients may want you to survey the site on this first visit, so it is wise to travel with your surveying equipment and a portfolio of pictures of work done for your previous clients. Clients often have an idea of what they do *not* want but are less clear about what they do want, and photographs and plans of other gardens make this easier to establish. Also, if you are fairly new to the profession, do not be afraid to admit it – your charges should reflect this and bluffing will only lead to later embarrassment!

When you arrive at the site, make notes on factors such as the locality – affluent or otherwise – the state of upkeep of the property – a clue to both the clients' personality and the available labour – the architectural style of the house and the age and period of the furnishings. The colour schemes, the pictures on the walls and even the kitchen will tell you a lot about the clients and their lifestyle. Look for any dominant features outside the house that you may wish to echo in the design of the garden.

Normally the client will walk around the garden with you, pointing out likes and dislikes, things that are to be retained or discarded. You may not necessarily agree with all of this, but the preferences of the client are part of your brief, and time spent now finding out potential problems and preferences will save disagreement later. Often it is wise to have a second walk round the garden alone, your attention no longer being distracted, to assess the potential and also to think through the most mutually advantageous way of carrying

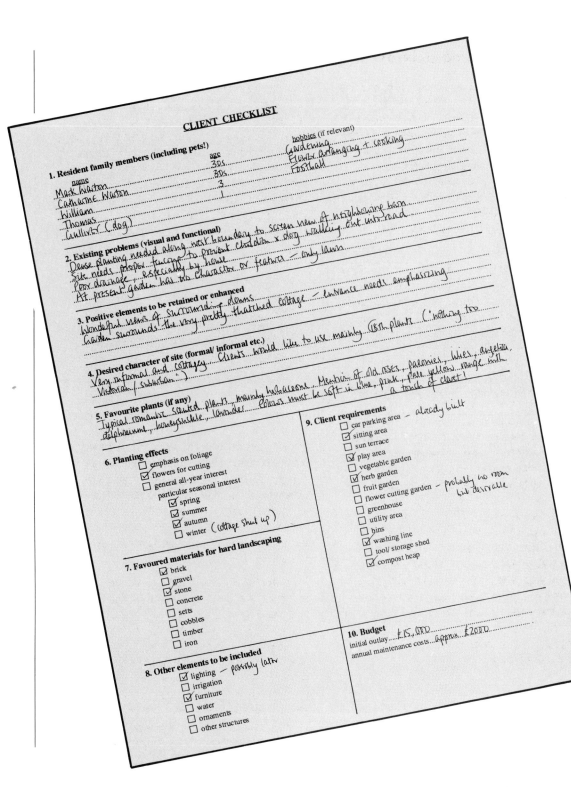

CLIENT CHECKLIST

1. Resident family members (including pets!)

name	age	hobbies (if relevant)
Mark Warton	30s	Gardening
Catharine Warton	30s	Flower arranging + cooking
William	3	Football
Thomas	1	
Gulliver (dog)		

2. Existing problems (visual and functional)
Dense planting needed along west boundary to screen view of neighbouring barn. Site needs proper fencing to prevent children & dog walking out into road. Poor drainage, especially by house. At present, garden has no character or features — only lawn.

3. Positive elements to be retained or enhanced
Wonderful views of surrounding downs. Garden surrounds the very pretty thatched cottage — entrance needs emphasizing.

4. Desired character of site (formal/ informal etc.)
Very informal and cottagey. Clients would like to use mainly 18th plants ("nothing too Victorian/ suburban").

5. Favourite plants (if any)
Typical romantic scented plants, mainly herbaceous. Mention of old roses, paeonies, lilies, angelica, delphinium, honeysuckle, lavender. Colours must be soft ie blue, pink, pale yellow range with a touch of claret!

6. Planting effects
- ☐ emphasis on foliage
- ☑ flowers for cutting
- ☐ general all-year interest
- particular seasonal interest
  - ☑ spring
  - ☑ summer
  - ☑ autumn (cottage shut up)
  - ☐ winter

7. Favoured materials for hard landscaping
- ☑ brick
- ☐ gravel
- ☑ stone
- ☐ concrete
- ☐ sets
- ☐ cobbles
- ☐ timber
- ☐ iron

8. Other elements to be included
- ☑ lighting — possibly later
- ☐ irrigation
- ☑ furniture
- ☐ water
- ☐ ornaments
- ☐ other structures

9. Client requirements
- ☐ car parking area — already built
- ☑ sitting area
- ☐ sun terrace
- ☑ play area
- ☐ vegetable garden
- ☑ herb garden
- ☐ fruit garden
- ☐ flower cutting garden — probably no room but desirable
- ☐ greenhouse
- ☐ utility area
- ☐ bins
- ☑ washing line
- ☐ tool/ storage shed
- ☑ compost heap

10. Budget
initial outlay... £15,000
annual maintenance costs... approx £2000

---

out the work. While it is essential to convince the clients that you know exactly how to deal with the garden, do not go into too much detail at this stage lest they carry out your ideas themselves without employing you.

Establishing a budget

A budget, or amount of money that the clients have available for the project, must also be established at an early stage. It may help to point out that a garden is like an outdoor room and that the budget allocated to it should be comparable to that set aside for an important room such as a kitchen. When it comes to establishing a budget your clients will want to know what they will get for their money. You should have a good idea of the costs of a range of materials as well as of the likely laying and maintenance costs of those materials. Try also to have a figure for planting costs per square metre (yard) that includes the plant themselves and any soil conditioners, fertilizers and so forth that may be necessary plus the cost of labour required to prepare the ground and do the planting. Obviously this figure will vary according to your sources of plants and the kind of planting that the clients require – for example, the proportion of shrubs to herbaceous plants – as well as local labour charges.

Once these matters have been agreed, a follow-up letter stating your objectives can then be sent, and if accepted, work can begin.

◀ **A checklist is useful to remind you of clients' preferences and the state of the site.**

3

The site survey

Before any serious work can begin on replanning a garden, an accurate survey of the site must be carried out so that a plan can be drawn up to show the existing situation. This plan should give the exact location of the various elements of the site indicating their height and width, and it should also show any changes in level. Although your clients may not wish to keep certain features, they should still be included in the survey, as any decision to retain, remove or re-site features will be made at a later stage.

The survey should include all measurable elements, not only the house and the boundaries of the garden, but also any features that may affect future planning – anything from drainpipes, manhole covers, electricity poles, changes in level, to existing trees and shrubs. It must also include notes on non-measurable elements, such as views out, orientation, prevailing winds, soil type and texture, all of which will influence the design and must be noted while on site.

The measured information will be used to draw up a scale plan of the site, and this plan will become the basis for all future work. It must therefore be accurate. If it is not, it could jeopardize any future plans by seriously distorting the eventual layout and probably inflating the cost of the garden unnecessarily. Clarity is essential when noting measurements, most mistakes being made by the measurer being unable to read or understand dimensions from his or her own notes.

A survey should include the following:

- **the house**, including doors and their direction of opening, and windows with sill heights .... ☐

- **existing man-made features** – drains, vents, wall plants and any other elements along or close to the house wall; outbuildings, such as garages or sheds, should not be overlooked .... ☐

- **boundaries** formed by hedges, fences or walls, including the material as well as the height, width and position of any uprights, buttresses or gates, or other access points or openings .... ☐

- **major trees and shrubs**, showing trunk, girth, height and spread, and names where possible .... ☐

- **low retaining walls, paths and steps**, including their direction, height and width, and the material used....................................... ☐

- **any areas of water** – pools, ponds, streams or lakes... ☐

- **existing planting** – flower beds, shrubs, trees or grass .... ☐

- **changes in level** resulting from slopes or terraces... ☐

- **drainage** – the position of manhole covers and, if necessary, the septic tank.......... ☐

- **the north point**, or direction of the sun at noon in relation to the site .... ☐

- **features outside the property boundaries that may affect the garden** – a neighbour's overhanging tree, for example ...... ☐

- **non-measurable elements**, such as views in and out, direction of prevailing winds, soil type and pH factor...................................... ☐

It is, of course, possible to have a professional survey done by a land surveyor, but this is expensive and you will learn a great deal more about the site by doing the measuring yourself.

Surveying procedure

It is best to begin by drawing an overall sketch plan of the site, on which all major features are noted. Spend some time investigating the site, walking around the boundary to familiarize yourself with the layout. Then return to the house to work out the procedure to be used on the particular site. It is usually easiest to start with the house and with elements close to the house, typically within a 5-metre (5-yard) range, before measuring more distant elements, such as boundaries and trees.

Taking the measurements

You will use a combination of your short and long tapes to measure the site. The rigid metal tape is straightforward to use and requires no explanation. The long tape, however, needs more careful handling. The easiest and most efficient way of using it is to keep the tape measure under your left arm (or right arm if you are left-handed) and to pay out or gather in the tape using your right hand. Between dimensions, treat the loose tape as if it were a coil of rope, looping it over your arm. Wind in the tape only when you have completed surveying an area. When you wind in the tape, do so through a damp rag or cloth, otherwise dirt will get into the case and the tape may jam.

Measuring the house and nearby elements

Sketch an outline plan of the house on a sheet of graph paper. Make it as large as possible but leave some room for writing in measurements around the side. Using graph paper helps to keep the proportions and relative positions of elements in the drawing reasonably correct, but do not attempt to draw the site to scale, unless it is very tiny, as this is rather time-consuming.

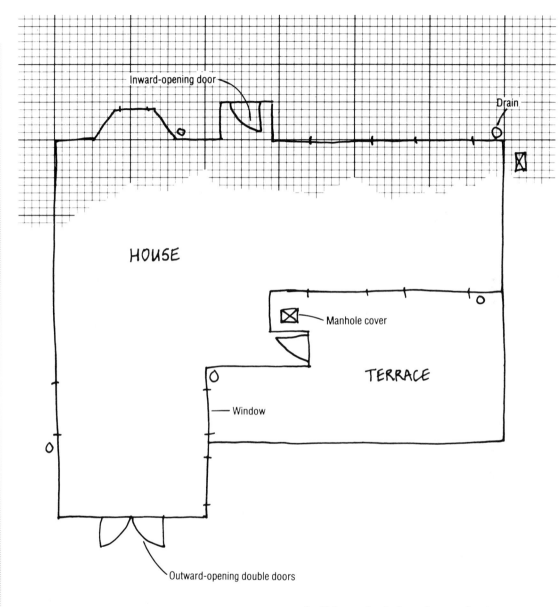

▲ **Using a sheet of graph paper, begin your survey by drawing the house and other close features.**

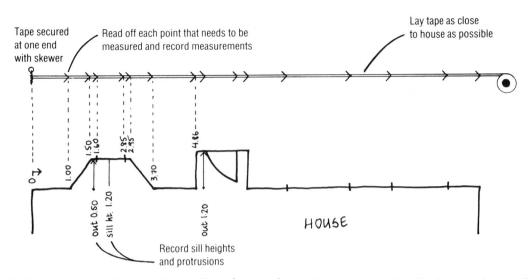

Tape secured at one end with skewer

Read off each point that needs to be measured and record measurements

Lay tape as close to house as possible

Record sill heights and protrusions

HOUSE

▲ **Measure each side of the house using running, or progressive, measurements.**

While you are doing this, note the position of windows and doors, and their direction of opening, and any elements close to the house, such as drains, manhole covers or nearby shrubs. If the site is a very small one you could include the boundaries and all existing garden elements on this first sheet of paper, but it is usually best to avoid cluttering one diagram unnecessarily and resketching the house outline for another plan can be done in a very short time.

You are now ready to start measuring each side of the house. Pay out your tape along the length of the house, as close to the house wall as possible. Then lay the reel down on the ground and go back to the beginning of your tape. This should line up with one corner of the house and be secured with a metal skewer or brick to ensure that it does not move. The tape must be taut and untwisted along its length before you start to read off any measurements.

Now, starting at the beginning of your tape, read off the position of all edges, doors, windows, taps, drains and so on along the house wall. This method of measuring, which is called taking running or baseline measurements, is quicker

and much more accurate than taking measurements by shifting the tape along. Mark the beginning point with O and an arrow to show the direction in which you are measuring. Try to record all subsequent baseline measurements with the figures orientated in the same direction. This should help to minimize the risk of confusing them with other measurements when you are drawing up the plan later.

When you have recorded all the horizontal measurements, use your rigid tape to take direct measurements of the heights of window sills, lights, taps and so on and of any indents or protruberances of the building. These measurements can be taken quite quickly by establishing a common base line as a datum, such as the horizontal damp-proof course.

You can also measure elements close to the house by using a combination of your long and short tapes. With your tape still running along the house wall, note how far along an element occurs, and then, using your short tape, note how far out it is from the house wall. This method of measuring is called taking offsets.

▶ **Using long and short tapes, take right-angle offsets to locate individual items close to the house.**

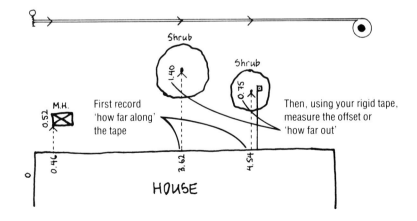

Shrub

Shrub

M.H.

First record 'how far along' the tape

Then, using your rigid tape, measure the offset or 'how far out'

HOUSE

Measuring more distant elements

When you have completed the house survey, take a fresh piece of graph paper and sketch on it the site boundary. Within this, draw in the house and any other elements that you wish to locate, such as trees, paths and garages. To ascertain their exact positions, you will be using a system of measuring called triangulation, which is used to locate a third point in relation to two known points or an established baseline. You can, for instance, ascertain the position of a tree by using as reference points two corners of the house that you have already measured. Simply measure and note down the distance from each corner to the tree. Back in your office, you can plot the measurements using a compass, as shown in the diagram.

▶ **From two fixed points A and B, use triangulation to locate distant elements, such as point C. Back in the studio a scaled drawing can then be produced from the measurements taken.**

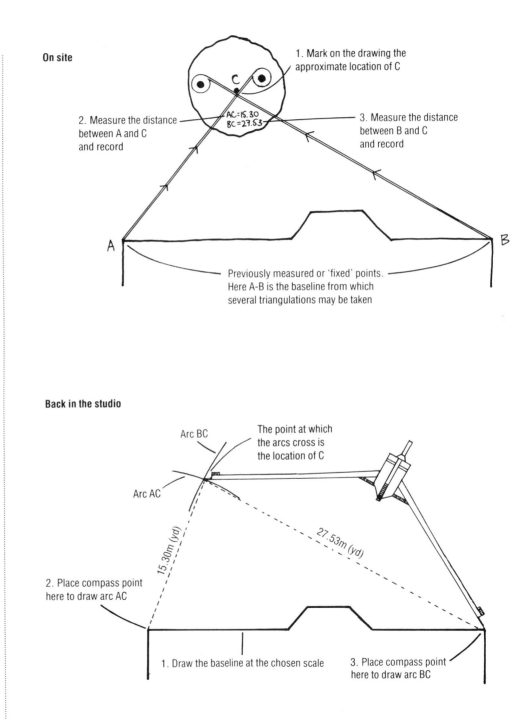

On site

1. Mark on the drawing the approximate location of C

2. Measure the distance between A and C and record

AC = 15.30
BC = 27.53

3. Measure the distance between B and C and record

A

B

Previously measured or 'fixed' points. Here A-B is the baseline from which several triangulations may be taken

Back in the studio

Arc BC

The point at which the arcs cross is the location of C

Arc AC

15.30m (yd)

27.53m (yd)

2. Place compass point here to draw arc AC

1. Draw the baseline at the chosen scale

3. Place compass point here to draw arc BC

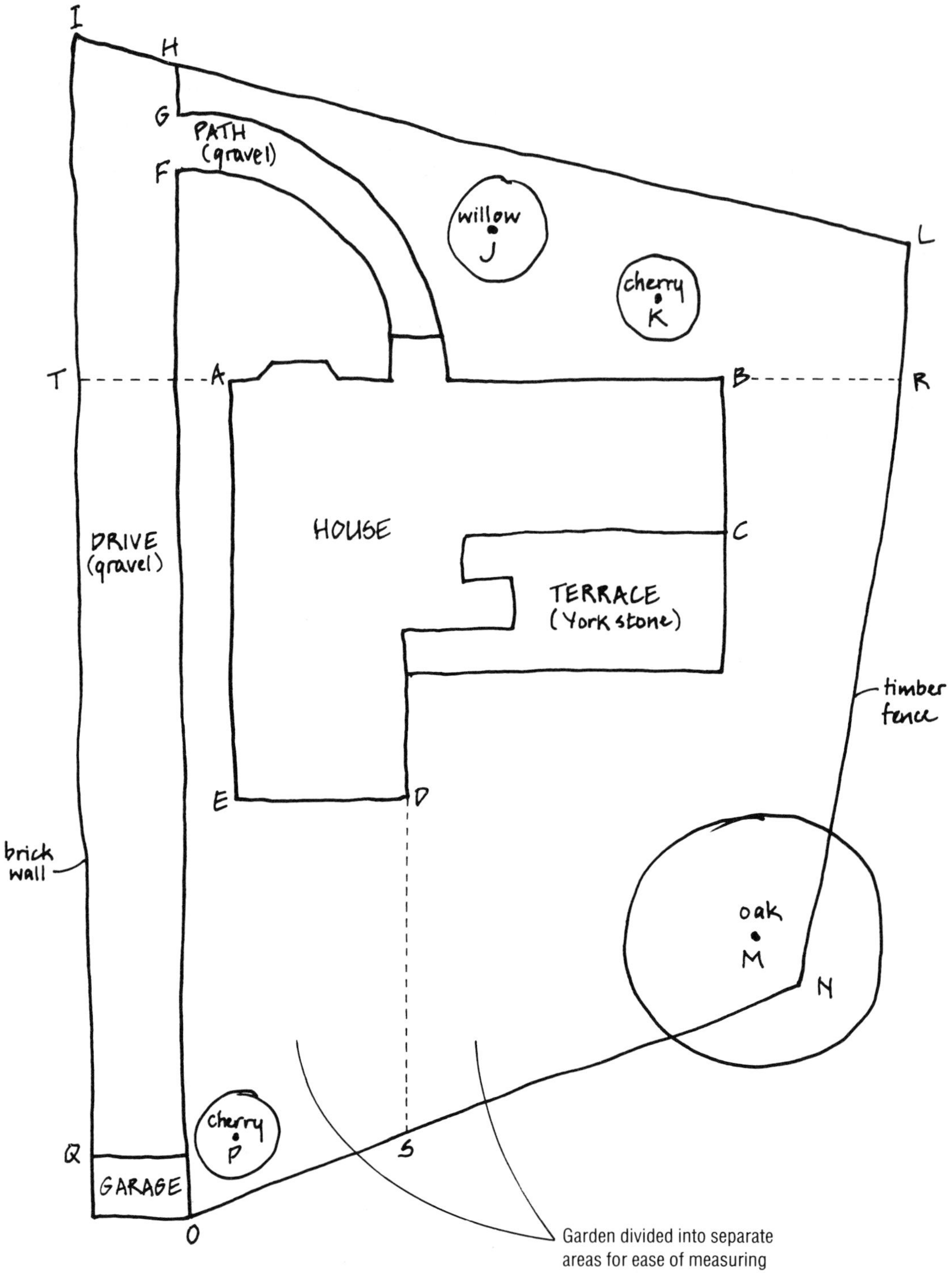

I

H

G

F

PATH
(gravel)

willow
J

cherry
K

L

T   A   B   R

DRIVE
(gravel)

HOUSE   C

TERRACE
(York stone)

timber
fence

brick
wall

E   D

oak
M

N

cherry
P

Q

GARAGE

O   S

Garden divided into separate
areas for ease of measuring

► **After drawing in the house, boundaries and other site elements, use capital letters to label the main corners of the house and all other relevant points to be measured.**

Before you start to measure it is often helpful to label on your sketch all the points that will need to be located and the known points from which they will be triangulated. Triangulation is very useful for establishing elements that are not parallel or at right angles to a building, such as paths and boundaries. Often they may appear to be so, but triangulating the points reveals otherwise! When you choose a baseline or two fixed points from which to measure, try to select the longest unobstructed line, from which all or most of the area can be seen. For most sites, however, particularly when the house is surrounded by the garden, you will need more than one baseline.

What appears to look like this

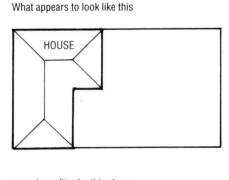

may, in reality, be this shape

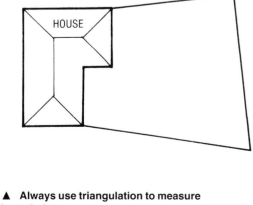

▲ **Always use triangulation to measure boundaries.**

When you are recording your measurements you may like to write the distances down next to the point you are trying to establish, or at the side of your drawing. If you first make a note of all the measurements you will have to take, you will reduce the risk of leaving the site without having completed your measuring.

▶ **To prevent your drawing from becoming cluttered and illegible, record all the elements as neatly as possible.**

Figures can be recorded either close to the relevant point on the sketch or at the side of the drawing.

If the distances to be measured are longer than your 30m (100ft) tape, you can use a ball of string to set out the line first. The measuring can then be tackled in stages. You may find it helpful to use garden canes or other markers placed at regular intervals, which can later be totalled up.

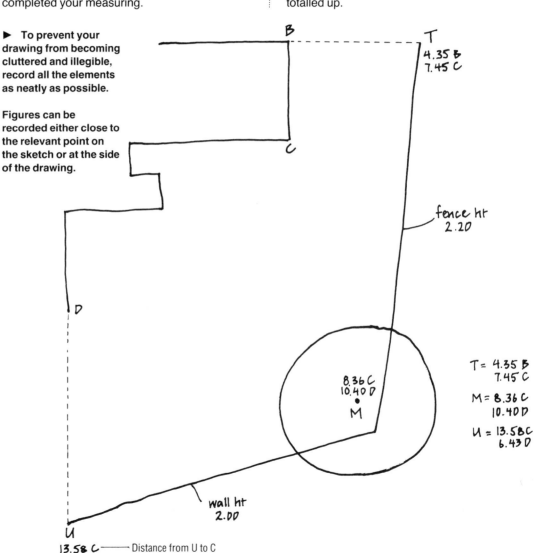

Measuring curves

Curves, such as curving paths, beds or boundaries are measured using offsets, taken at regular intervals from a baseline or a triangulation line. When taking an offset measurement you must ensure that it is taken at 90° to your baseline. You may find it useful to use a rectangular object, such as a piece of cardboard, to make the right angle.

The clock method for surveying small gardens

This technique is especially useful for small, fairly cluttered gardens, in which objects may obstruct the view from one corner of the plot to another. In this case, the baseline is formed by two garden canes, placed centrally, but some distance apart in the garden. Starting at one corner of the house, walk around the garden in a clockwise direction labelling every point that you wish to measure, ending up with the garden canes themselves. At the side of your drawing list all the distances from each of these points to the first cane, and then from each of these points to the second cane, not forgetting to note the distance between the two canes. Securing the end of your tape measure to the first cane you can now quickly rotate around the garden, recording all the measurements, and then do the same from your second cane.

▶ In the systematic clock method of surveying measurements can be taken and recorded quickly.

▶ Use a combination of triangulation and offsets to measure a curved path.

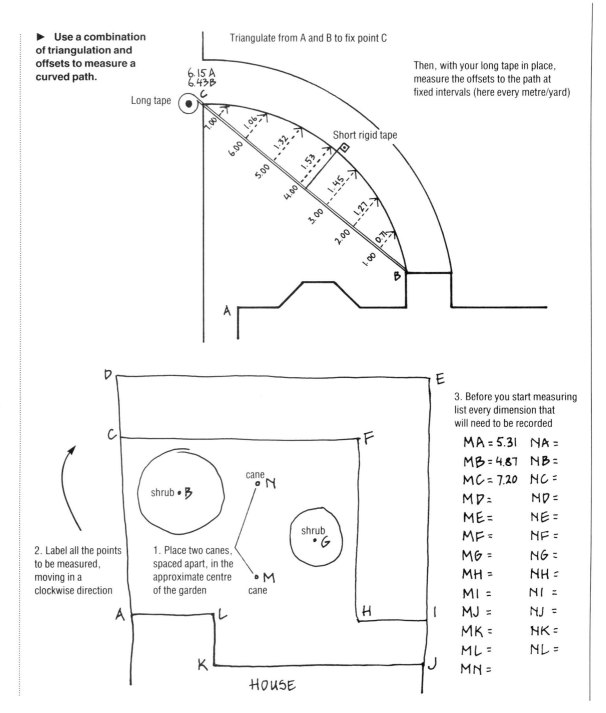

Triangulate from A and B to fix point C

Then, with your long tape in place, measure the offsets to the path at fixed intervals (here every metre/yard)

3. Before you start measuring list every dimension that will need to be recorded

MA = 5.31   NA =
MB = 4.87   NB =
MC = 7.20   NC =
MD =   ND =
ME =   NE =
MF =   NF =
MG =   NG =
MH =   NH =
MI =   NI =
MJ =   NJ =
MK =   NK =
ML =   NL =
MN =

2. Label all the points to be measured, moving in a clockwise direction

1. Place two canes, spaced apart, in the approximate centre of the garden

HOUSE

Measuring slopes or changes in level

Few sites are absolutely flat, and it is beyond the scope of this book to explain how to take levels using a theodolite and staff. However, it is possible to work out simple levels by using a spirit level, pegs and a plank. Start at the top of a slope and choose some level, permanent feature, such as a manhole cover, low retaining wall or step, and measure out from it a distance rather less than the length of the plank. At that point, drive in a peg so that its top is approximately level with the height of the permanent feature. Place the plank on the peg and rest a spirit level on it. You may need to adjust the peg until the spirit level shows a true level reading. Then measure the vertical distance between the plank and the slope.

Alternatively, simply squat down beside some permanent feature, such as a low wall, and compare by eye how much the ground, or any object rises or falls over a given distance. This will enable you to estimate the gradients. Counting the number of brick courses can also be helpful as a check on heights.

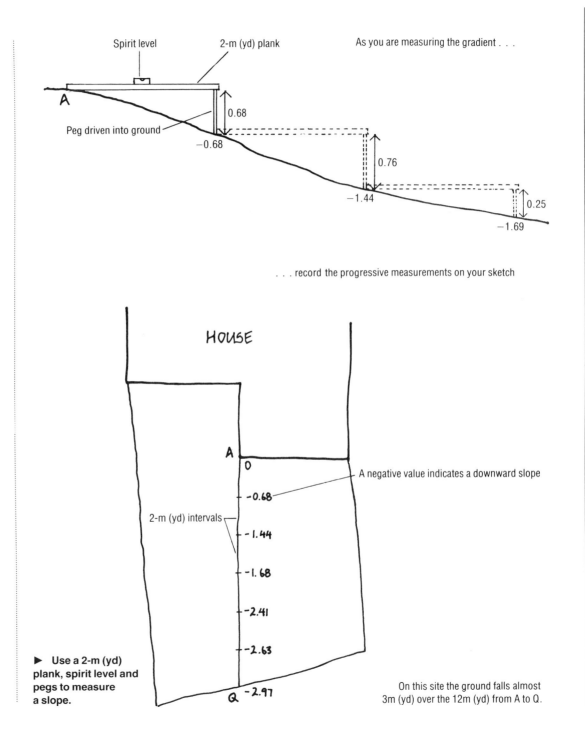

Spirit level   2-m (yd) plank   As you are measuring the gradient . . .

Peg driven into ground

0.68

−0.68

0.76

−1.44

0.25

−1.69

. . . record the progressive measurements on your sketch

HOUSE

A negative value indicates a downward slope

2-m (yd) intervals

A
0
−0.68
−1.44
−1.68
−2.41
−2.63
Q −2.97

▶ Use a 2-m (yd) plank, spirit level and pegs to measure a slope.

On this site the ground falls almost 3m (yd) over the 12m (yd) from A to Q.

Measuring trees or large shrubs

In addition to naming each tree, there are five measurements that may need to be recorded:

- the centre of the trunk
- the diameter (or girth) of the trunk
- the width or spread of the tree canopy
- the height of the lowest branches
- the overall height of the tree

Having located the centre of the trunk by the triangulation or offset method, both the diameter or girth and the canopy spread can be estimated by using a tape laid on the ground. To estimate the height of the lowest branch and the overall tree height, it is useful to have an assistant. Ask him or her to stand by the tree and work out, using your assistant's height as a guide, how many times the height goes into the lower branches and the overall height. If you do not have an assistant, find some other object with a known height, such as a garden building, and work out the height from that reference point. Mark in these dimensions alongside the centre of the tree.

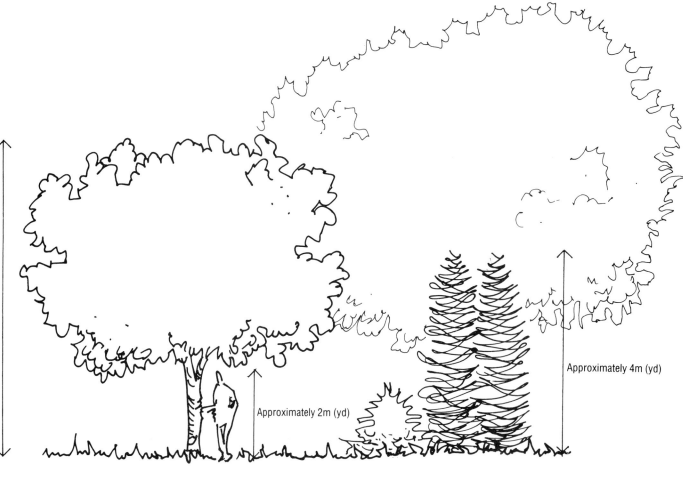

Approximately 6m (yd)

Approximately 2m (yd)

Approximately 4m (yd)

► **Use the height of a person as a reference to estimate the height of trees.**

Soil type or pH factor

The existing vegetation may give you a clear indication of the soil type. Some plants, such as rhododendrons, camellias, heathers and other ericaceous plants, prefer acid soil or soil that is low in lime, nitrogen and phosphate, but in which minerals such as manganese are available to the plant. Acid soil, which is rich in iron, often occurs in rural areas that are, or were, heavily wooded, and where leaves and other debris have, over the centuries, created a thick layer of decomposing material, which has interacted with soil and subsoil to produce damp, peaty conditions.

Alkaline soil is unable to provide iron, manganese and boron in a universally acceptable form, and plants that require these minerals are unable to exist in these conditions.

The acidity or alkalinity of the soil is measured on a pH scale, which varies from pH1, very acid, to pH14, very alkaline. Plants vary in their degree of tolerance to high and low pH, and although most will grow on soil that is close to neutral (pH7), an indication of the soil type must be established before any serious planting can begin. It is always wise to test the soil, and you will need to collect a small amount from a range of points representative of the overall site. You may find the soil differs in various parts of the garden.

To do this you will need a trowel, small polythene bags, labels and a pen. Decide at which points the soil should be taken – under trees, in open ground, at the base of walls, for example – and mark these points as SS1 (soil sample 1), SS2 and so on on the survey. Use the trowel to take about a tablespoonful of soil from approximately 100mm (4in) below the surface, tip it into a polythene bag, label the bag and tie it securely. When you get back to your office, tip the soil onto saucers and place each one on top of the now empty, labelled bag, and allow it to dry out naturally before testing with a soil-testing kit.

Alternatively, send the samples to a soil-testing laboratory. The findings will later be recorded in the analysis of the site.

While you are taking samples for pH purposes, you will also need to consider the soil texture – the relative proportions of sand, silt and clay that the soil contains.

A less messy, but less accurate, method of testing soil is to use a soil meter, which can be pushed into the ground to give an immediate reading.

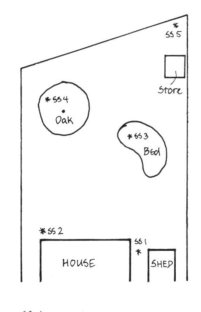

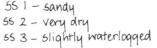

SS 1 – sandy
SS 2 – very dry
SS 3 – slightly waterlogged

▲ **When taking soil samples (SS), note their location and number the samples accordingly. Also note the condition and texture of the soil.**

Recording non-measurable details

You will now have written down many measurements, but before you return to your office or studio, there are many non-measurable factors to be taken into account.

A garden cannot be looked at in isolation – it must be considered in the context of its surroundings, and every site, however small or confined, is in reality a part of some larger whole with which it interacts, affecting and being affected by this wider environment.

Some of these factors may be visual, such as views within the garden, from the house, terrace or other vantage points, lawns or the architectural style of the house or even architectural details, like existing wall copings, which may be incorporated into a new wall design, or they may be to do with the climate or even the character, sound and smell of the site. The qualitative characteristics of existing features, such as the materials from which they are made, should also be noted – a brick wall which is in need of repair, for example.

In addition to revealing what lies within the boundaries, the survey must examine what lies beyond. This is called the zone of visual influence, and it may extend no further than the backs of houses in the next street or it may reach to a stretch of public footpath on a distant hillside. However near or far, the zone must be defined before any real consideration can be given to design. Certain rooms within the house may give distant views, and you should stand at the windows and do a quick sketch or take a photograph of what you can see. Select vantage points outside the house – a terrace or some sunny area where the client may wish to sit, for instance – and do another quick sketch. Only outline shapes are necessary and speed is important, for you will often be surveying in bad weather with fading light.

Orientation

All plans for the garden should take into account how the position of the sun affects the garden. Unless the weather is really bad, you can easily do this by looking to see the position of the sun at the time of your visit and working out where it will be at noon. Usually the owners of the garden will also be able to tell you, but you can check the exact orientation by using a compass or looking at a street plan or map.

When you draw a plan you should always indicate the north point. Remember, too, that the amount of sun or shade that a garden receives will vary – in winter the arc of the sun is lower, making shadows wider and deeper, while in summer, although the sun is higher, deciduous trees in full leaf can cast shade.

Climate

The climate will affect the way in which the garden is designed and used. The site location, aspect, altitude, topography and temperature will all have a bearing on the site, and should be noted at this stage – a seaside garden will be affected by wind and salt spray, for example, which will mean that only plants tolerant of these conditions can be used.

The direction of the wind can also render certain parts of the garden unusable. This may not be apparent on your particular visit, so you should ask the client or find out from a local weather station or airport. In some situations, wind speeds can be increased by being 'funnelled' between high buildings, while obstructions can direct the wind, causing it to blow from unexpected quarters.

You should also be aware of the possible existence of a microclimate within a garden. The climatic conditions within particular defined spaces can vary considerably from the average

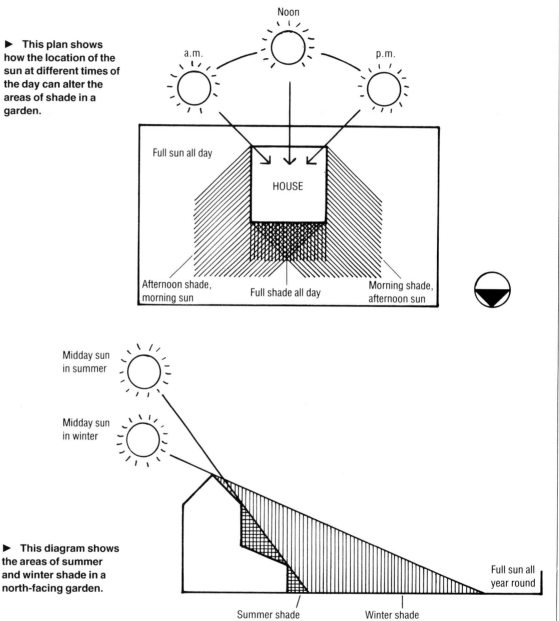

▶ **This plan shows how the location of the sun at different times of the day can alter the areas of shade in a garden.**

Full sun all day

HOUSE

Afternoon shade, morning sun

Full shade all day

Morning shade, afternoon sun

Midday sun in summer

Midday sun in winter

▶ **This diagram shows the areas of summer and winter shade in a north-facing garden.**

Summer shade

Winter shade

Full sun all year round

local climate. For instance, if a garden is on a windy hillside but is surrounded by high walls, the area immediately in the lee of these walls will be sheltered, but the more open space beyond will still be subject to wind.

Site inventory

Every site will have its own limitations, which will affect design proposals. Go through a site inventory before you leave the site. Some of the points will not be relevant while others that are not on the list may be raised, but all the information must be noted down while you are on site and transferred to a site analysis at a later stage.

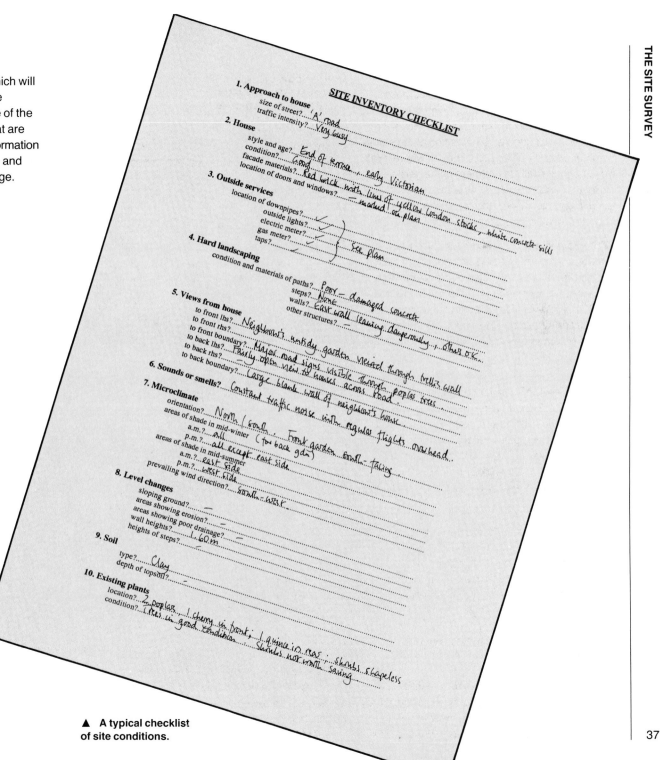

SITE INVENTORY CHECKLIST

1. Approach to house
size of street? 'A' road
traffic intensity? Very busy

2. House
style and age? End of terrace, early Victorian
condition? Good
facade materials? Red brick with lines of yellow London stocks, white concrete sills
location of doors and windows? — marked on plan

3. Outside services
location of downpipes?
outside lights? ✓
electric meter? ✓ See plan
gas meter? ✓
taps? ✓

4. Hard landscaping
condition and materials of paths? Poor — damaged concrete
steps? None
walls? East wall leaning dangerously, others O.K.
other structures?

5. Views from house
to front lhs? Neighbour's untidy garden
to front rhs?
to front boundary? Major road signs visible through poplar trees
to back lhs? Fairly open view to houses across road
to back rhs?
to back boundary? Large blank wall of neighbour's house

6. Sounds or smells? Constant traffic noise with regular flights overhead

7. Microclimate
orientation? North (south. Front garden south-facing
areas of shade in mid-winter (for back gdn)
a.m.? all
p.m.? all except east side
areas of shade in mid-summer
a.m.? east side
p.m.? west side
prevailing wind direction? south-west

8. Level changes
sloping ground? —
areas showing erosion? —
areas showing poor drainage? —
wall heights? —
heights of steps? 1.60 m

9. Soil
type? Clay
depth of topsoil? —

10. Existing plants
location? 2 poplars, 1 cherry in front; 1 quince in rear; shrubs shapeless
condition? trees in good condition; shrubs not worth saving

▲ **A typical checklist of site conditions.**

Using a camera to record data

A camera is invaluable for recording site information. Often there is so much information to be noted that the naked eye, however well trained, overlooks some detail – an unsightly light fitting, overhead telephone cables, the condition or state of existing walls – and even obvious lines and shapes may not have been apparent while you were on the site itself. Such features will be revealed on a photograph, which you will be able to study carefully in your studio.

Photographic prints can be used as a basis for a report on the garden, as a reminder of the site itself or as a basis for quick overlays of sketches to show how the garden might look if replanned. Old photographs can indicate the historical background or use of a site, and aerial photographs can reveal previous ground patterns or the outlines of former planted beds. The appearance of the garden before, during and after replanning can be recorded to build up a photographic portfolio of successful projects to show future clients or the camera can be used simply to show seasonal changes as the garden develops.

To record information successfully, photography should be approached systematically. If photography is to be at all helpful, you will need to have an adequate camera and lens. A 28mm wide-angle lens is especially useful for panoramic views, but almost any camera will do. The photography will often be left until after all the other site information has been gathered, by which time the light may be fading or shadows distorting the views, so film speeds of ASA 200 or 400 may be necessary. Colour print film is usually the most useful for recording the site, but occasionally a report on a garden can be very effective when it is illustrated with black and white photographs, although they are more expensive and take longer to develop than colour.

Keep several spare rolls of film cool in a domestic fridge ready for site visits to save a last minute dash to a photographic supplier and to ensure that the film colour and quality stay fresh.

Types of photographs
The main categories of photograph that will be required are:

- panoramic views from the house
- views of, and back to, the house from the far end or boundary of the garden
- close-ups of specific items and their condition – terraces, walls, pergola, conservatory, existing planting and so on.

Using the methods outlined below will enable you to have a complete photographic record of the site. When they have been developed the prints should be clearly labelled with the client's name and address and the date on which they were taken. They can then be filed or mounted above your desk or drawing board for future reference.

Panoramic shots Begin with panoramic views from the house. Choose a central position – often a doorway – and standing with your back to the house and using your body as a pivot shoot first to the far left-hand side, while carefully noting what is in the far right-hand side of the picture frame. Take the second shot by just including in the left-hand side of the frame what was seen in the right-hand side of the previous frame. Continue by moving around clockwise in a half-circle or circle, keeping the camera as steady and level as possible – a tripod will help – until you have completed the panoramic view. Occasionally it may be necessary to take a near, middle and distant panorama to show plantings, buildings and boundaries in sufficient detail.

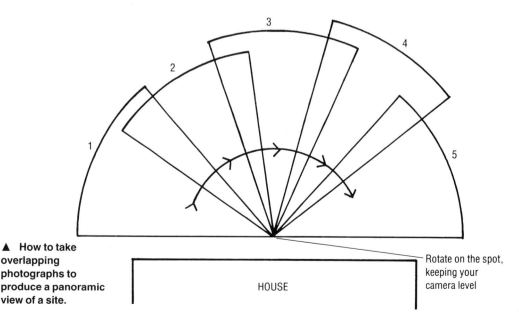

▲ How to take overlapping photographs to produce a panoramic view of a site.

HOUSE

Rotate on the spot, keeping your camera level

▼ The resulting panorama, made by overlapping each photograph.

Views of the house Next move to the opposite end of the area or to an imaginary line some distance from the house to take the views of, and back to, the house. Set up this imaginary 'line' and move along it from left to right, again using the 'overlap' system.

This method will give you a 'flat' view of the house or building, which as well as being a useful basis for an overlay or sketch of what the house and garden may look like after replanning, will also provide a record of the position of doors, windows, downpipes and so on. If the site is very large, it will need to be sub-divided into different areas, similar to the measured areas for the survey, each of which will be treated separately.

The best views of a small garden and its surroundings are often captured by photographing from an upstairs window. This will enable you to look down onto the site and to include adjacent gardens, houses or other buildings. The scene will alter from summer to winter – a sycamore tree that is in leaf and casting heavy shade on the garden may be hiding the view of an unsightly factory or handsome church spire, while in winter, when the tree is bare, the garden may appear sunny and light but be overlooked.

Close-ups of existing features Finally, walk round the site and take close-ups of anything you particularly want to record. These may be a severe crack in a wall, poor drainage on a terrace or a badly shaped tree. Often the reason for your photograph will be to point out to the client the need for repair or removal!

Aerial photographs
If the site being worked on is of particular historical significance, it may be useful to obtain or commission aerial photographs of the site. These are best taken in dry weather because

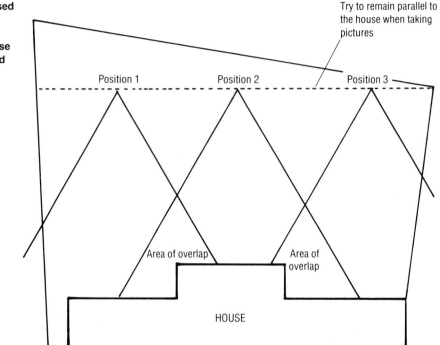

▶ **The technique used to take photographs from the house and views back to it. These are useful as a record and as the basis for overlays.**

Try to remain parallel to the house when taking pictures

Position 1   Position 2   Position 3

Area of overlap   Area of overlap

HOUSE

previous groundworks will show more clearly in drought. There are a number of specialist firms that have picture libraries or that can arrange the photography for you. Occasionally pictorial records may be obtained from magazines or research libraries.

Uses of photographs
If you intend to publish articles or books you may need photographs to accompany text, and publishers require colour transparencies, rather than prints. You may, therefore, wish to take additional photographs for this purpose. Alternatively, you may simply want to keep a photographic record of the gardens as they develop. It is always interesting to compare 'before' with 'after', and it is an effective way of impressing future clients.

▲ **The resulting elevation.**

Photographs can be used in many ways by designers, and with experience a designer soon comes to appreciate that time spent recording the site on film may save hours of work later. This list gives some further possibilities:

- as a record of the site prior to work beginning, during construction and after the work is completed
- to prove the need for specialist work – tree surgery, site drainage and so on
- as a check when measurements have been forgotten – heights of walls can be calculated by counting up the number of brick courses, for instance

- to record certain plants or plant groupings
- to reveal previous site usage or ground patterns, although aerial photographs are best for this purpose
- to use as a complete 'panorama' of the site to be pinned above your desk as a reminder
- to use as a basis for quick 'before' and 'after' sketches or for perspective drawings
- to record particular details for later reference – downpipes, trellis work, plant groupings and so on
- to show seasonal differences
- to build up a design portfolio of completed work.

Once the photographs have been taken and the film developed, you can decide how best to use them. If you are using the 'panorama' method, the photographs should be overlapped, stuck down and mounted on to card to fix on a wall above your drawing board for easy reference. If they are to be used in a report or for sketching over, some views can be selected and duplicates made. If necessary, the photograph can be enlarged to a suitable size on a photocopier and then sketched over using tracing paper.

Photographs can also be stuck round the site inventory and analysis sheet to clarify certain comments.

Photographs are the best way of recording any existing features that the client wishes to retain in the new garden design. Unusual items, such as this rustic bench, may well inspire or restrict a future design theme.

When surveying a garden a camera is useful for recording details like those shown here: a roof terrace overlooking the garden, a sagging wall and a specimen tree to be retained. A photographic record of work in progress can be shown to future clients, so that they can see how a garden develops.

4
Drawing up the site plan

The survey must now be drawn up to scale. This drawing will become the base plan and, because future design work will be carried out by tracing over it, it must be an accurate representation of the site. Even if the site is an awkward shape, the outline drawing should fit comfortably on a standard size sheet of paper, with enough space for additional notes or drawings. The outline must also be sufficiently distinct to be visible through several sheets of tracing paper.

Setting up the equipment

Before you can begin any drawing you will need to set up a work place. This should be equipped with an anglepoise lamp, set to shine from left to right if you are right-handed, and the drawing equipment listed in Chapter 1.

Make sure that your drawing board is set at a comfortable angle and that your parallel motion or T-square is parallel. Begin by securing a backing sheet of gridded graph paper to the drawing board with masking tape, checking that the horizontal lines on the sheet correspond to the parallel motion or T-square. Similarly, check by using a set-square, held firmly against your parallel motion or T-square, that the vertical lines also correspond. Once it is stuck down, the backing paper will serve for months as a guide to setting up a drawing, for lettering and for general layout, so it must be positioned correctly. The chosen size of tracing paper should be positioned on top of this and also secured with masking tape at the corners. The survey notes can now be drawn to scale on this sheet.

Choosing the scale

The purpose of a scale drawing is to produce an accurate representation of the garden on paper, with everything shown in its correct position. This scale drawing will act as a basis for all the following steps in the design process. In reality the garden is rarely seen from this 'overhead' view, unless from an aeroplane, but it is necessary to work on a plan so that one can see at a glance how each object or space relates to another. Because a successful garden design relies heavily on the relationship of one area to another, an accurate plan must be the basis for future design work.

On any scale rule you will find series of ratios – 1 : 1, 1 : 10, 1 : 20, 1 : 50, 1 : 100, 1 : 200 and so on – representing different scales. The largest scale is 1 : 1, which represents a reproduction of the same size as the original. If the drawing is reproduced at 1 : 10, it will be 10 times smaller.

In garden design the most often used scales are 1 : 50, 1 : 100 and 1 : 200, which are used for both garden layout plans and for planting plans.

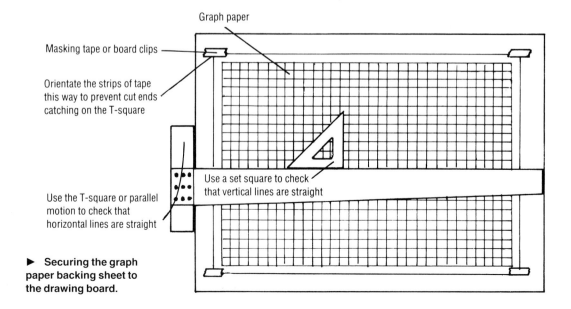

Graph paper

Masking tape or board clips

Orientate the strips of tape this way to prevent cut ends catching on the T-square

Use a set square to check that vertical lines are straight

Use the T-square or parallel motion to check that horizontal lines are straight

▶ **Securing the graph paper backing sheet to the drawing board.**

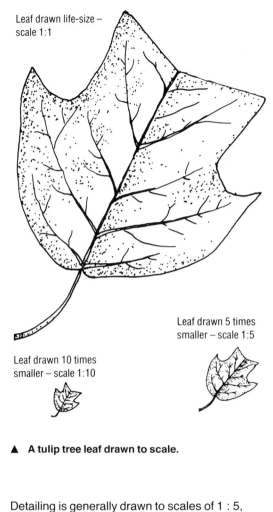

Leaf drawn life-size – scale 1:1

Leaf drawn 5 times smaller – scale 1:5

Leaf drawn 10 times smaller – scale 1:10

▲ **A tulip tree leaf drawn to scale.**

Detailing is generally drawn to scales of 1 : 5, 1 : 10, 1 : 20 or 1 : 50. Cartographic maps are usually drawn to scales of 1 : 1250 and 1 : 2500, and they are really only of use in garden design in determining points such as the orientation and precise location of a site.

Drawing the survey up to scale is always an exciting task, and it should always be done as quickly as possible after the site visit, as notes are always easier to read while they are still fresh in the mind.

Sometimes, when you are plotting the measurements, it becomes obvious that a dimension has either been noted down incorrectly or has been overlooked entirely. If it is discovered immediately, the client can be asked to check the vital dimension or the site can be revisited. This is less easy if the mistake is found only three weeks later and two days before the plan is due to be finished.

The survey can be drawn up on various sizes of paper, but to produce a professional design from which printed copies can be made the final layout plan will need to be drawn on tracing paper, which is normally available in standard sizes, ranging from A4 (11⅔ × 8¼in) to A0 (46¾ × 33⅛in). Most gardens will be drawn up on A2 (23½ × 16½in) paper, but if the garden is large or if a lot of detail, such as paving steps or intricate planting, is to be shown it may be better

to work to a larger scale on a larger sheet as A1 (33⅛ × 23½in). If the garden is an awkward shape, the outline may need to b moved around before it will fit on to the sheet. It is also easier and less expensive to reproduce smaller sheet sizes. Although there is much work to be done before you can commit yourself to your final paper size, there is little point in drawing up the survey to scale, only to have to enlarge or reduce it later.

Begin by measuring and drawing to scale first the overall length of the garden and then its overall width. Will these overall dimensions fit comfortably onto your intended sheet size, or will the site plan take up all the available space or appear too large or too small? When you choose a scale or size of paper try to find a balance, making sure that you can show all necessary details without having to draw up a huge plan.

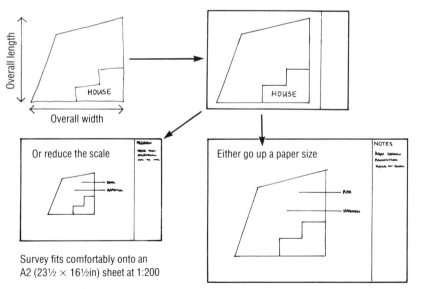

A quick sketch of the site drawn to a scale of 1:100

Overall length

Overall width

Survey only just fits onto an A2 (23½ × 16½in) sheet, leaving inadequate space for labels and notes

Or reduce the scale

Survey fits comfortably onto an A2 (23½ × 16½in) sheet at 1:200

Either go up a paper size

NOTES

Survey fits comfortably onto an A1 (33⅛ × 23½in) sheet at 1:100

▲ **Paper size and the scale to be used for drawing up the survey need to be considered together.**

Drawing the site plan

When you have selected the scale to fit the chosen size of tracing paper, or vice versa, the survey measurements and notes can be plotted on the tracing paper to make an accurate survey drawn to scale or a site plan. Even though this survey will mainly be used as a basis for later drawings, it should still be placed centrally on the sheet, with ample space left for notes around it.

When you draw up the site plan it is logical to proceed in exactly the same order as you chose to survey the site, beginning with the base line of the house and working out from that until the boundaries have been completed. In trying to decide which way to place the survey, it may help to think of the client's main viewing points of the garden and to set the plan at a similar angle. When drawing, always use a well-sharpened pencil or clutch pencil, because blunt leads can give inaccurate dimensions, and try not to smudge the graphite by working over it with your hand. Use a duster or drawing board brush to keep your work clean and free from eraser rubbings.

Begin by drawing the house at the chosen scale and then use compasses to locate the boundary, a tree or another building. In many cases the distance measured will be longer than the stretch

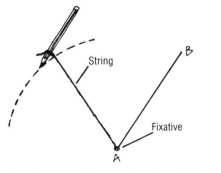

▲ **If a dimension is longer than the stretch of your compass, use a piece of string with a pencil attached to make the arc.**

of the extension arm and therefore difficult to locate accurately, but it can be achieved by using a combination of scale rule, string and pencil – perhaps a slightly Heath Robinson approach, but nevertheless effective. You may wish to use a beam compass, but this is quite an expensive item.

Continue moving round the site on paper as on the actual site until all measurements have been transposed. Tick off each dimension as it is plotted as a check on what has already been done. In some cases, an absolutely accurate rendering may not be easy – points may not quite join up, for example – and therefore a little artistic licence may be allowed. However, if the dimensions do not meet, or are seriously out, it may be wise to revisit the site to check them.

When you are plotting trees, show the actual position of the trunk and the spread of the canopy, including a note of the overall height and, if known, the botanical and common names. Shrubs or other plants that may play a significant part in the new design should similarly be indicated. The heights and thickness of walls, measurements of the treads and risers of steps and the overall dimensions of any other relevant artefacts should also be shown, as should manhole covers, septic tanks and if known, the drainage system and the level of the damp-proof course (DPC). Problems arising from the location of these items may affect the design, and although they can be talked through on site with the contractor, there is no point in disregarding their whereabouts at this early stage.

The first pencil-drawn survey is usually fairly messy, the sheet being punctured with arcs and pin pricks from your compasses, and it may, therefore, need to be retraced to make it more legible. Take a further sheet of tracing paper, stick it down over the drawn survey and trace

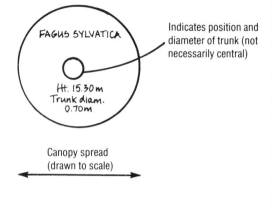

▲ **How to show existing trees on a plan.**

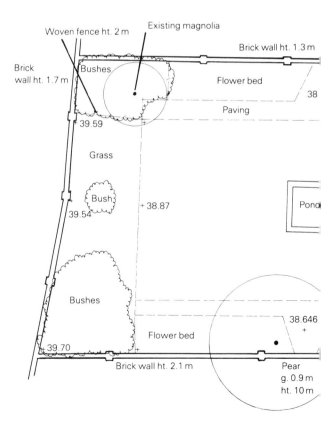

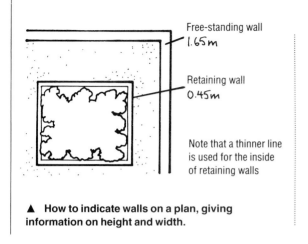

Free-standing wall
1.65m

Retaining wall
0.45m

Note that a thinner line
is used for the inside
of retaining walls

▲ **How to indicate walls on a plan, giving
information on height and width.**

over it in pencil or, preferably, ink because this is darker and easier to read through several sheets of paper as the design is being worked up.

Finally, in the bottom right-hand corner, insert the north point, the scale at which the survey has been drawn, the address of the property and the date on which the drawing was finished. Note that putting both the name and address of the client has not been suggested, so that some degree of anonymity can be preserved. Your name, address and telephone number should also be included.

This drawing will now become the site plan, from which the new garden layout will emerge. It will show the existing elements on site and will be used as a basis for the site analysis. For this reason it is occasionally also referred to as a base plan, but the term site plan is now more commonly used.

▼ **A professional site
survey, showing spot
heights.**

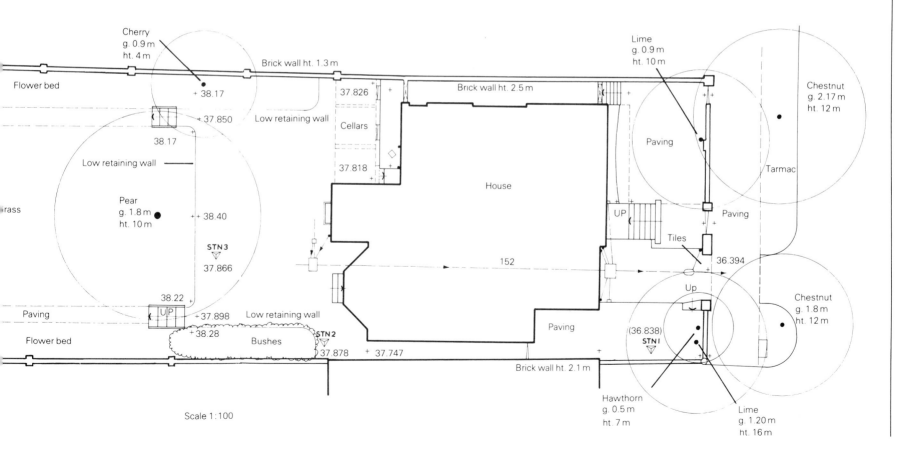

Scale 1:100

5

The site inventory and site analysis

The site inventory and site analysis are two interim stages between drawing up the site plan and beginning the design. These drawings are very rarely seen by the client, but they are a means by which the garden designer gains an understanding of the problems and potential of a particular site.

For various reasons, the design or construction work cannot always begin immediately, and the inventory is a factual description of the state of the site at the time of the survey, to which you will refer frequently when you are initially planning the new design. Usually the constraints and limitations of a site outweigh the advantages, but both must be taken into account. Sometimes a client may wish to alter or revise a particular aspect of the completed garden layout plan, contrary to the designer's advice. Referring back to the inventory and analysis will serve to jog your memory and remind you of your reasons for deciding on a particular design and enable you to explain your motives for handling the project in a particular way.

The simplest way to prepare the inventory and analysis is on two separate drawings, which can be made as tracing paper overlays to the site or base plan. Alternatively, you could use a copy negative of the base plan to save any redrawing (see page 127). The first drawing, the inventory, is an accurate factual account of the current state of everything within, and immediately without, the site, and it should be compiled from the notes taken on the survey visit – 'boundary wall in poor condition, brick coping deteriorating', 'lawn mostly moss/little grass evident' or 'old pear tree showing dieback/disease on some branches', for example. Positive features, too, should be included – 'fine views to distant hills', for example – until all features within the garden have received comment. Remember to include the immediate surroundings, and notes taken on site may reveal comments such as 'distant view partially obscured by overgrown sycamore'.

Whenever information can be most simply expressed as graphic symbols, use them to help bring the plans to life. You may, for instance, like to use blue hatching to denote damp or windy, exposed areas or yellow stars for sunny, warm areas.

► A site inventory provides a record of existing features and the state of the site.

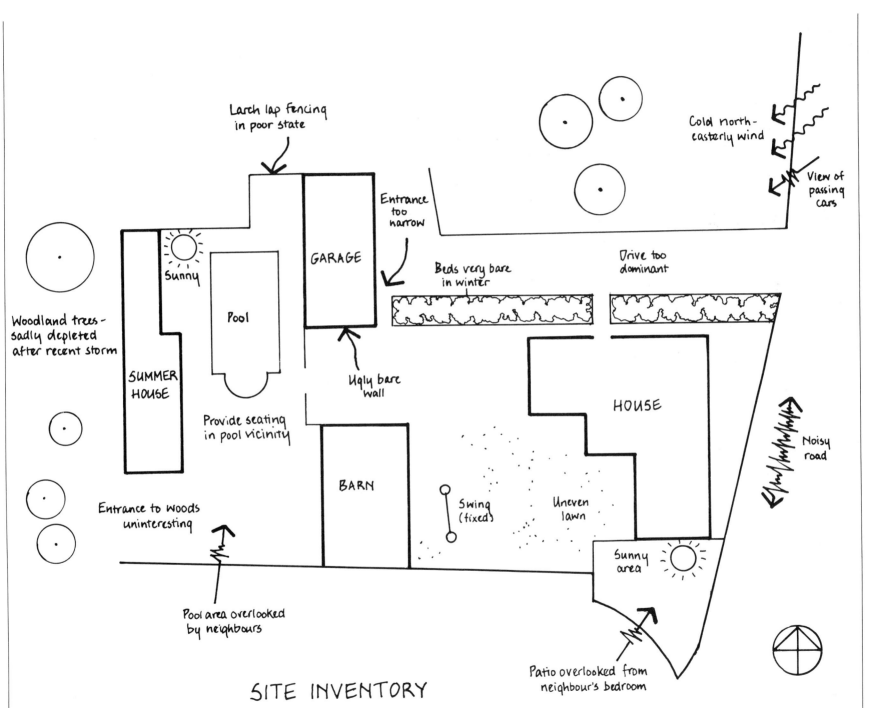

Larch lap fencing in poor state

Cold north-easterly wind

View of passing cars

Entrance too narrow

GARAGE

Beds very bare in winter

Drive too dominant

Sunny

Pool

Woodland trees - sadly depleted after recent storm

SUMMER HOUSE

Ugly bare wall

HOUSE

Provide seating in pool vicinity

BARN

Swing (fixed)

Uneven lawn

Noisy road

Entrance to woods uninteresting

Sunny area

Pool area overlooked by neighbours

Patio overlooked from neighbour's bedroom

SITE INVENTORY

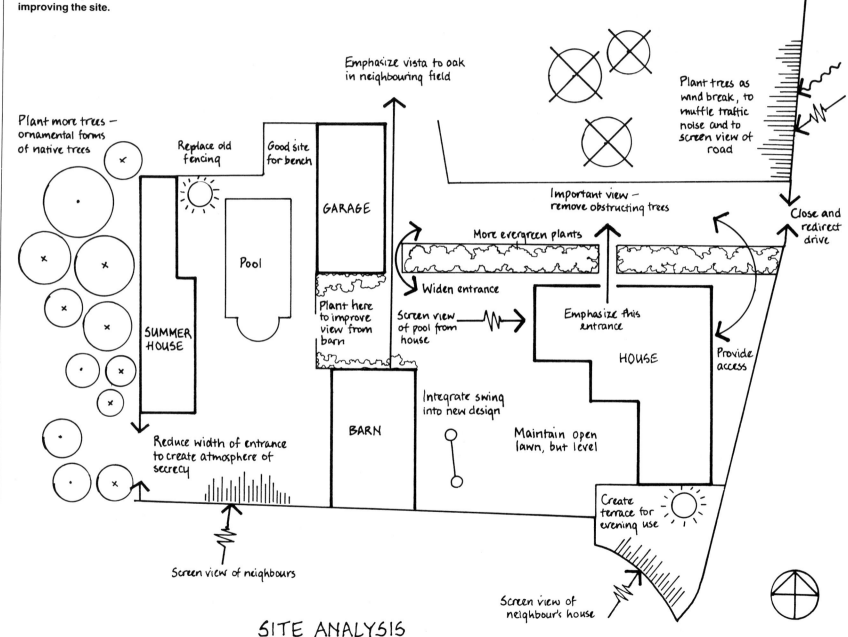

▼ This analysis suggests ways of improving the site.

Plant more trees — ornamental forms of native trees

Replace old fencing

Good site for bench

Emphasize vista to oak in neighbouring field

Plant trees as wind break, to muffle traffic noise and to screen view of road

GARAGE

Important view — remove obstructing trees

Close and redirect drive

More evergreen plants

Pool

Widen entrance

Plant here to improve view from barn

Screen view of pool from house

Emphasize this entrance

Provide access

SUMMER HOUSE

HOUSE

Integrate swing into new design

Maintain open lawn, but level

BARN

Reduce width of entrance to create atmosphere of secrecy

Create terrace for evening use

Screen view of neighbours

Screen view of neighbour's house

SITE ANALYSIS

The second sheet, the site analysis, should evaluate the importance of the information on the inventory by looking at ways of solving the problems and by taking advantage of the potential offered by existing site conditions – 'remove overgrown sycamore to reveal distant view' or 'plant hedge to obscure view of neighbour's shed', for example. Although these drawings will not generally be seen by the client, there are occasions when plans have to be put before a committee, which may require a clear, simple proposal to help it reach a decision. In this case it is best to have the site inventory and analysis complete with notes printed or photocopied and then to add colour for emphasis and clarity. The removal of trees, for instance, is always an emotive subject, and those trees under threat can be circled in red to show their precise location and so facilitate an informed discussion of the reasons behind the proposed removal. With practice and imagination, the site inventory and analysis can become an informative and colourful document that provides a summary of the requirements and, to some extent, the intent of the design. The inventory and analysis can also accompany a report.

► **A sketch on tracing paper laid over a photograph is a quick way of showing clients how their garden can be transformed.**

Writing a report

A report is often the final step in the research and preparation phase. It is seldom necessary for a small garden, but for a larger garden it is an invaluable method of summarizing the state of the existing garden, making proposals for improvements and providing the basis for future design work. It is a useful way of beginning a large and lengthy project, and it should contain enough information for constructive discussion and to help the client and designer decide how and when to proceed with implementing the plan.

The report should be compiled in the same way as the site analysis and appraisal, but, because it is normally used for larger gardens, estates or commercial developments, it is easier to break the site down into different areas and to comment on each particular area, possibly discussing in each case such items as paving, paths, steps and walls, tree planting and decorative planting. Often, for ease of referral, a report will need to be accompanied by a scale survey of the entire site, with each area divided up to correspond with the areas in the report.

Photographs can be used to illustrate some points, and the photographic method of illustration can be taken further by doing a tracing paper sketch as an overlay – a quick and easy 'before' and 'after'. If the 'after' is drawn carefully in ink it can then be printed on clear acetate or left on tracing paper to give a clear, impressive, yet simple way of illustrating, for instance, how the view will alter after the removal of the sycamore tree.

It is important not to give away too many design ideas at the report stage, or clients may try to implement them themselves. A report should entice your clients into employing you. It can also be used to explain the motives behind a design to associated professionals, such as architects working on a hotel complex or other large-scale work, and copies of it can easily be made to give to the various people concerned in such a development.

6

Developing the design

Now that the site plan, inventory and analysis have been completed, you are ready to begin working up the design. This is a daunting stage, and being confronted with a completely blank, pristine sheet of tracing paper, which should soon contain a new garden plan, can induce panic in the most seasoned designer. Often an uninspiring or difficult site can render the designer devoid of inspiration. One way out of this is to create a grid, using existing site lines, and then to experiment with abstract patterns and shapes which frequently reveal an entirely new concept. These shapes can then be linked to the existing site using the grid. This should ensure that the eventual design proportions are pleasing and well balanced.

The bubble diagram

Long before you start to think of the style of garden you intend to create or of decorative details or planting designs, you must decide where you are going to place all the elements you intend to include in the garden and how these are going to function. At this point you will find it useful to have your clients' checklist and site analysis close to hand. Your clients may, for example, want a herb garden, in which case you must decide where in the garden would be the best place for this. If your clients intend to use the herbs for cooking you may at first think of placing the herb garden near to the kitchen. However, when you look at the orientation of the site, you may find that this part of the garden is very shaded and is, therefore, unsuitable for growing the many culinary herbs that require the sun. So you have to look at an alternative position. When you have found a suitable location for the herb garden, you must decide what is going to go next to it. Perhaps it would be pleasant to have the barbecue terrace here or the ornamental pool – or would this be the ideal place for the potting shed?

To help you decide what to put where, use a bubble diagram, drawn freehand on a sheet of tracing paper and laid over your site plan. Draw different sized bubbles, corresponding to all the elements and the space that you need to include in your design, making sure that you do not leave any gaps between the bubbles that you cannot identify.

These simple, functional drawings represent an exploratory stage of the design process and, being quick to complete, should enable you to look at many alternative sites for all the different elements in your new design.

► **This bubble diagram indicates roughly the proposed position of all required elements, the amount of space they will occupy, and how they will relate to domestic use.**

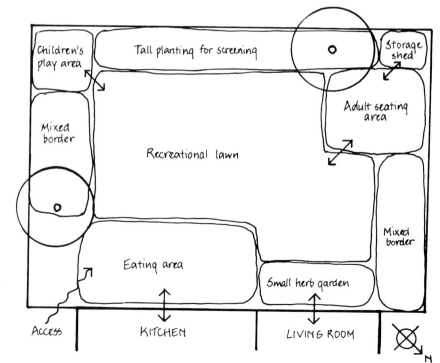

The grid system

Once you know roughly what is going where and how much space you will need to allocate to the constituent elements of the garden, you are ready to start designing or to start converting your rough bubbles into specific shapes with defined edges. To help you get the proportions right, you may find it helpful to use a grid, which you should evolve from your site plan. The grid lines that you draw should spring from dominant lines in the site, such as the outside walls and corners of the house, protruding bays or extensions or wall buttresses. Using these existing structures to influence where new elements should go will help to coordinate old and new features.

In deciding how to divide up the site, look at the dimensions between the dominant site lines to see if they fall into some sort of module. You may, for instance, find that the distance from the corner of the house to the extension is 2 metres (2 yards), the distance from the extension to the next corner is 4 metres (4 yards) and the

protrusion of the extension is 2 metres (2 yards). In this case a 2-metre (2-yard) grid would be ideal. For a larger house you may choose larger grid squares, following the rule that the scale of the grid should derive from the mass of the property. Many formal houses were built to a strict module of, say, 3 or 5 metres (3–5 yards), but in many cases new doors, windows or extensions have been added with no reference to the original module. In these instances you will need to experiment with your scale until you find a suitable way of dividing up the space. In some cases the module may not spring from the house itself but from some other features within the site, such as paths or gates. If the site is virgin land – perhaps simply a field surrounded by a fence – you can measure the entire length, say 30 metres (30 yards), and width, say 18 metres (18 yards), and simply divide it into equal sections, which in this case would give you a choice of a 6-, 3- or 2-metre (6-, 3- or 2-yard) grid.

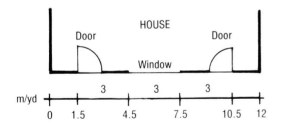

◀ **The dominant features of the house suggest a 3-m (yd) grid.**

▶ **The grid should be drawn up on tracing paper laid over the site plan.**

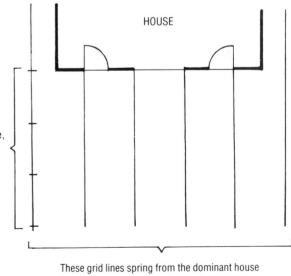

From the corner of the house, the cross lines continue across the garden

These grid lines spring from the dominant house features, such as the door, walls and windows

If the site is large, you may wish to have a smaller grid, say 3 metres (3 yards) around the house, which can be doubled or trebled where the garden moves out into more open landscape. A square grid is much easier to use than a rectangular one, particularly if you are developing a circular theme for the design. Avoid the temptation of using graph paper squares as a basis for your grid – these are unlikely to correspond to dimensions that spring from the site itself, which is the main objective of this system. By basing your design framework on a grid, each area will be related to others in size, shape and proportion, giving cohesion and unity to your design.

Draw up your grid on tracing paper laid over your site plan. Once you have decided on the scale of your grid, use your parallel motion and set-square to draw in all the lines, both vertical and horizontal, to cover the whole area of the site.

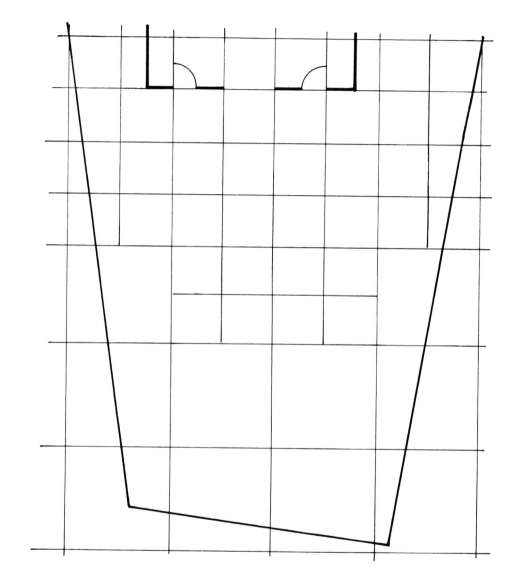

► **The 3-m (yd) grid becomes a 6-m (yd) grid as it bleeds out into the landscape, encouraging larger, more natural shapes further from the house.**

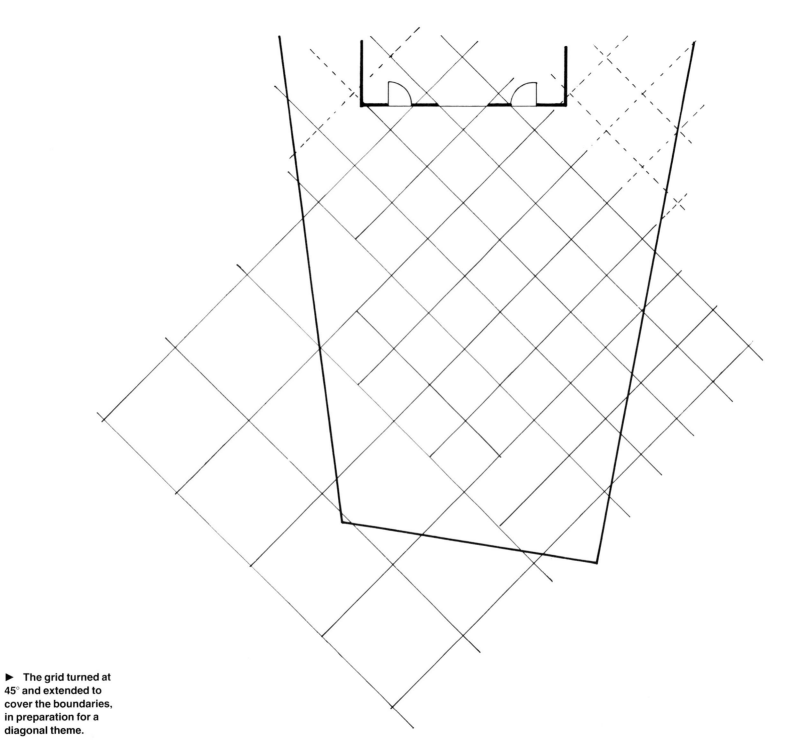

▶ The grid turned at 45° and extended to cover the boundaries, in preparation for a diagonal theme.

Creating patterns

With the grid in place you are now ready to try out different design themes based on geometric forms, such as circles and squares. If you are an inexperienced designer you should, at this point, temporarily abandon your bubble diagram and with it any preconceived ideas of how the garden should be laid out. What you are going to do now is to experiment with shapes of different sizes to produce several pieces of abstract art that you find visually and aesthetically pleasing.

Lay a fresh sheet of tracing paper over your site plan and grid and draw in different shapes or parts of shapes (straight lines, diagonals and curves), using the grid lines to help you position your shapes within your site and to determine their sizes, which should cover more, but not less, than one grid square. If you find it difficult to know where to start, try using cut-out shapes, which again should be multiples of your grid squares and which you can first arrange then draw around. Different shapes can combine effectively provided they have a strong relationship, one shape springing from the dominant line in another. The way in which you combine these forms will be the basis of the garden's character, and the more you practise using and combining shapes, the more you will appreciate how different shapes have qualities that you can use to give a garden a feeling of order, informality or boldness. You will find that some of your patterns are static and restful, while others are more exciting and have a sense of movement.

When you have created several patterns with which you are happy, you can experiment with these. Try rotating and reversing your patterns, or shading certain areas to divide your garden into positive and negative space, or into areas of mass and void. All gardens are a combination of mass and void, but it is the proportion of the one to the other that is significant. One-third mass to two-thirds void is often an effective ratio.

► By tracing over a few selected lines, these interlocking shapes can be the basis for numerous other designs.

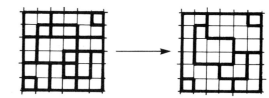
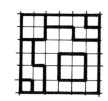

► In the search for an interesting design solution a pattern can be (a) rotated (b) reversed (c) turned at 45°.

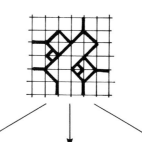

a   b   c

► Experiment with alternative combinations of mass and void.

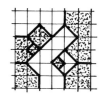

Experimenting with shapes should help you to create totally fresh and new ideas to redesign a site, rather than simply tinkering with what is already there and readjusting it. Inspired with different ways of using the space, you are now ready to turn back to your bubble diagram and see how you can adapt your patterns to accommodate all the different elements required.

Introvert and extrovert gardens
The garden designs tend to fall into two categories – the introvert garden, in which the interest is concentrated within the garden, by blurring the boundaries with planting, and the extrovert garden, in which the eye is encouraged to move beyond the garden boundaries to focus on attractive distant features, such as buildings

or trees. On occasion, particularly in towns, one side of a garden may be overlooked by neighbouring houses, while the other side enjoys an open, sunny view. In this case, the attention may be concentrated on that open view, with the less attractive aspect being treated as in an introvert garden, possibly disguised by a trellis or a thick band of planting.

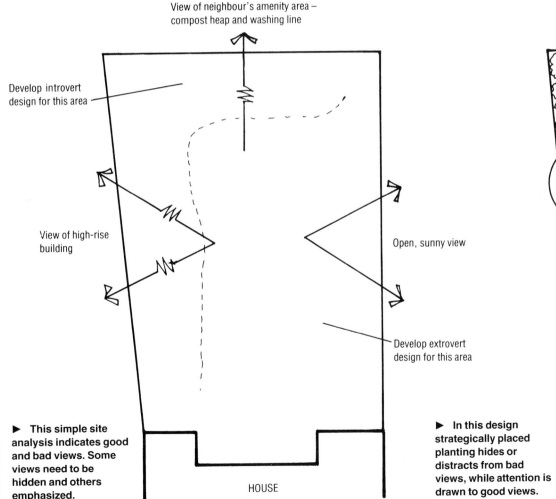

View of neighbour's amenity area – compost heap and washing line

Develop introvert design for this area

View of high-rise building

Open, sunny view

Develop extrovert design for this area

▶ **This simple site analysis indicates good and bad views. Some views need to be hidden and others emphasized.**

HOUSE

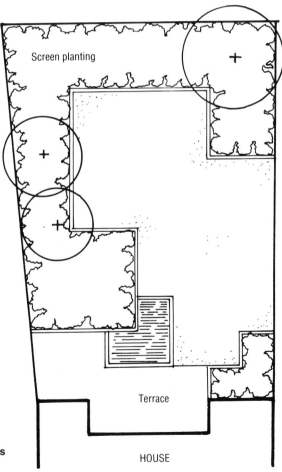

Screen planting

▶ **In this design strategically placed planting hides or distracts from bad views, while attention is drawn to good views.**

Terrace

HOUSE

Static and dynamic designs

The choice of a particular design theme will depend on which is most appropriate for the site. The architectural style of the house may dictate whether the garden is to be formal or informal. Circular or strong, geometrical patterns may work well for small gardens, which usually require an introvert design. Small gardens are usually seen from the house as one complete picture, which must look good throughout the year, with everything from hard landscaping through to planting, pots and garden furniture earning its keep. The design may be static or have a sense of movement.

▶ **This informal, dynamic design has a sense of movement.**

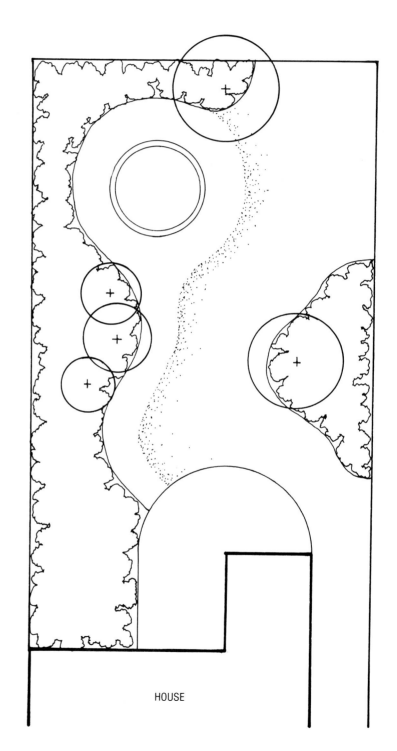

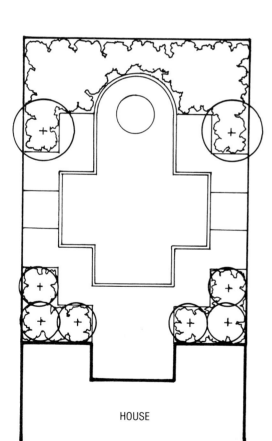

HOUSE

◀ **The simple shapes in this plan for a formal, static garden could be interpreted in numerous ways, depending on the material (water, paving, statuary, etc.) that is chosen for each space.**

HOUSE

Diagonal themes

Long, thin gardens can often benefit from using a diagonal design, which draws the eye from one side of the garden to the other, helping to create an illusion of width. Frequently the garden can be divided into three equal spaces, with the diagonal layout aiding movement from one space to another. A similar sense of movement can be induced by using bold curves, with carefully placed trees acting as pivots to balance and alter the directional flow.

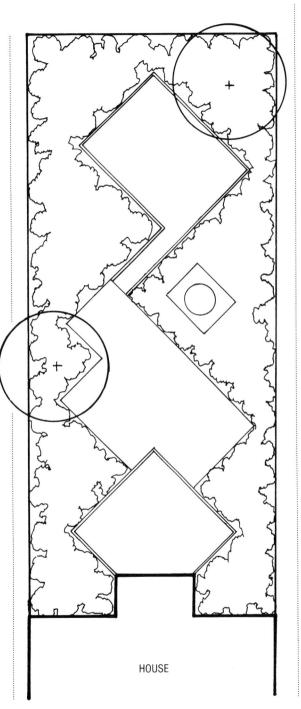

► A diagonal design theme – which makes use of the longest stretch of the garden – creates an illusion of width.

HOUSE

Translating your pattern into a preliminary design

Horizontal and vertical planes

Although you are creating a flat plan, you must try to think of your garden as a three-dimensional object. Unless some interesting features or trees are to be retained the garden will appear very flat. You may wish to break it up by creating a change in level by using paths and steps to move from one space to another. Or you could include some raised beds with retaining walls, or pergolas, arches, urns, pots and so on. Then, of course, there are the plants, most importantly the trees. When they are carefully sited trees can hold the horizontal plane together, balancing the flat spaces and acting as a pivot to turn corners or change direction or simply to lead the eye and encourage a sense of movement through the garden. Think also about the rest of your planting – not about the types of plants you intend to use but about their general height. You should label these areas as high, medium and low planting.

Relating your plan to the human scale

Once you are happy with your general design concept, you must start to refine your drawing, looking carefully at each element or space to make sure that the dimensions allowed for them will work practically and are properly related to the human scale. You should be asking yourself such questions as: Have I left enough space for a comfortable arrangement of chairs on the terrace? Are the paths wide enough? Have I allowed sufficient room for a car to turn on the drive?

You may well have to adjust the dimensions slightly, abandoning your grid which, by this stage, will have served its purpose and can be put away.

You will now have some idea of how you wish the finished garden to look, but you may not know how to show this on a plan, perhaps being

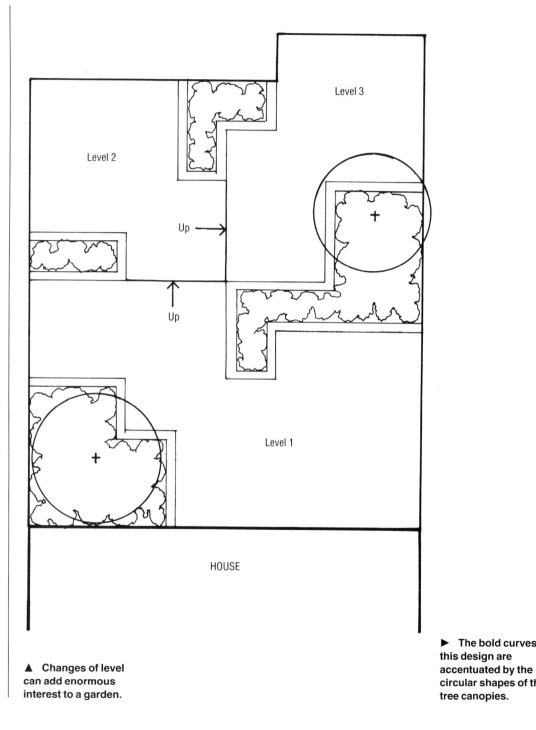

Level 3

Level 2

Up

Up

Level 1

HOUSE

▲ Changes of level
can add enormous
interest to a garden.

► The bold curves of
this design are
accentuated by the
circular shapes of the
tree canopies.

HOUSE

unsure of how much space to allow for structures such as paving, paths and pergolas. There is really no standard rule, the main factor being to allow enough space for the adult body, whether singly or *en masse*.

A simple way of relating the scale of a plan to the human frame is to draw a 'pin' man to scale beside the drawing. This can then be quickly measured to see how many times it will relate to the terrace or lawn. Think also about the machinery that may be required to build and maintain the garden. Similarly, if the only access is through a narrow alley, large artefacts or mature trees may prove a problem unless they are carried through the house. Too often, designers or architects repeat interior dimensions in the garden, the effect being mean and cramped, as the landscape is seen on a much larger scale.

When you are representing hard and soft materials on a plan, the scale at which your plan is drawn will affect how much detail you are able to show. If a plan is drawn to a scale of 1 : 200 or 1 : 100, it will be necessary to rely on written, descriptive information rather than a graphic representation, and the actual drawn details of the construction will be provided separately. It is unwise to show anything on a plan that is not drawn to scale – paving stones, for example – as it is likely that your builder may simply scale off from your plan. If the paving stones have been drawn to a larger size, he could order extremely large slabs, that would be out of proportion with the rest of the garden.

The following points should be considered when you are planning the space.

Terraces or paved areas These are often adjacent to the house and are used to link house and garden. The materials and construction are expensive, and to save money terraces are frequently smaller than is aesthetically pleasing. A terrace should derive its proportions from the bulk of the house. By taking the height of the eaves and measuring this out on the ground, a successful balance can be achieved. Some allowance for planting may be required immediately adjacent to the house, and the terrace may, therefore, need to be projected out further.

Paths Often an edging, similar to the border of a carpet runner, is necessary to finish off a path visually. If necessary, additional space should be allowed for plants to flop over the edges, and in this case 1.5m (5ft) is necessary and will permit two people to walk almost abreast. Subsidiary paths can go down to 0.9m (3ft), but this will mean that people would have to progress in single file.

Ample room for parking and turning is necessary for drives and forecourts, the normal width for a drive being 3.5m (12ft), although it rather depends on whether the car is a Rolls Royce or a family saloon and how many visitors with similar cars will also wish to pass or park on the driveway.

Steps in the garden should have shallower risers and wider treads than an interior staircase. This will make the going easier. Steps should also be as wide as possible, with the tread overhanging the riser to give a cast shadow or delineation, for both appearance's sake and for safety. Steps can also act as pivots or to change the direction of paths.

If, when you visit gardens, you carry a tape measure with you to measure steps, you will be able to note down what feels and looks comfortable.

Water When you include artificial ponds or areas of water you must also make provision for water to circulate, the size of the pump being in proportion to the amount of water involved. Perhaps a fountain or lake complete with island and landing stage is envisaged. Dealing with water can be a problem, so do not hesitate to call in expert advice for large or complex projects.

Pergolas must always lead somewhere, the main criteria being that adults can walk comfortably under them, which means that the verticals must be at least 2.5m (8ft) high. If they are placed close together, they will appear even higher. An average spacing is about 3m (9ft), but much will depend on the material used. Sturdy brick or stone columns, perhaps supporting timber beams or railway sleepers, can be spaced further apart than more flimsy metal arches. Space should also be made for the plants, both at the base and up and across the verticals.

Ground shaping or slopes Ground shaping or creating contours and levels must also be considered before the main work begins. Your survey may include spot levels, which indicate the height at the point (spot) at which they are taken. If they do not, you may need to ask advice. Earth-moving machinery may need to be employed. Isolated contours or mounds can look self-conscious and suspicious, as if they are trying to conceal something that the builder has left behind. It is far better to run proposed contours back into existing ones and to remove the excavated soil from the site.

7
Presentation of plans

The purpose of a plan, be it garden layout or planting, is to communicate your ideas to your client and ultimately to the contractor. If the client is being charged professional rates, he or she will expect a confident, professional drawing to which the garden can be constructed or planted.

At this stage your garden layout plan is a rough pencil drawing, probably on inferior quality tracing paper. When you present it to your client you will have refined it and retraced it onto the final sheet, which, apart from containing the plan, will be supplemented with vital written information and enhanced with graphics. This final sheet will be copied and coloured up before it is presented to your client.

When you are starting out as a garden designer you will need to design this final sheet, first for one paper size and then adapt it to fit other commonly used sizes – A1 (33⅛ × 23½in), A2 (23½ × 16½in) and A3 (16½ × 11⅔in) are the most useful. Once you are satisfied with these prototypes, you can have them printed in quantity so that you will have pre-printed sheets ready for use on future jobs.

Each final sheet, which should be drawn on superior quality, 120gsm tracing paper, will need to contain the following:

- a title block
- an information panel
- a border

These three items will remain constant, with the variable information, such as the client's name and the garden layout plan to be filled in later.

Title block

The basic information to be included in a title block is:

- your name or company title, address and telephone number
- your client's name or address
- drawing title (layout plan, planting plan, etc.)
- drawing number
- the scale or scales
- revisions
- date
- drawn by (initials only)
- statement of copyright
- disclaimer

The title block can be ornate or simple, depending on your own style. You may choose to include a logo to identify your work, to hint at a particular style or to be witty or amusing, but usually simple, clear title blocks are the most effective.

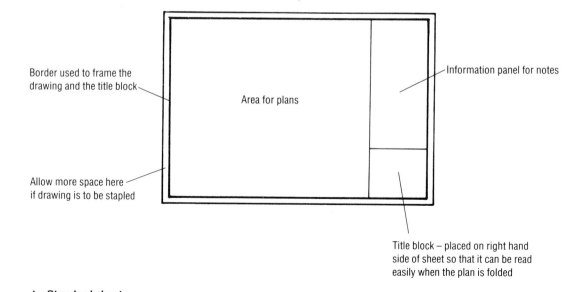

Border used to frame the drawing and the title block

Area for plans

Information panel for notes

Allow more space here if drawing is to be stapled

Title block – placed on right hand side of sheet so that it can be read easily when the plan is folded

▲ **Standard sheet layout for drawings.**

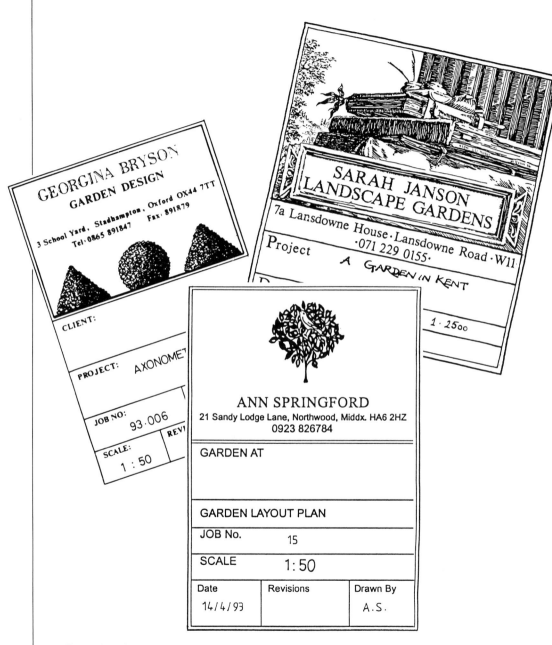

The title block should always be placed in the lower right-hand corner of the information panel and should be approximately one-sixth to one-quarter of the overall height of that panel. The location is important because when the drawing is printed, it will be folded, and the title block must always appear uppermost. Choosing the style and size of the lettering or type face and selecting different sizes and spacing is a personal matter (see also page 17). Your choice will depend partly on your clientele and on how polished you wish to appear.

You may like to make your own name stand out by using dry-transfer lettering for it, and then use stencils or freehand writing for the other variable information, adding this in ink each time.

An alternative to having a whole pre-printed sheet is to have the title block printed on adhesive sheets which can then be applied to a drawing, the changing details then being inked in later. These adhesive sheets are normally printed in reverse and need to be stuck on to the back of your sheet, with the changing information being written in on the front. Study the given examples and the notes on lettering, and experiment until you find an effective layout for your title block. If this all sounds complicated, ready-printed architects sheets can be purchased from most reprographic stores, but they do not have the individuality of a personal design.

Scale

A statement of the scale or scales used on the drawing should appear within the title block, shown simply as 1 : 50, 1 : 100 and so on. If there are several drawings of different scales on a sheet, the words 'as shown' may be written instead of the actual scale employed. The scale will then be shown clearly under each individual drawing. If the drawing is later reduced or enlarged, the statement of scale will no longer be

▲ **Examples of different styles of title block.**

accurate, and may then need to be altered or omitted. However, if a graphic scale is employed, this will remain accurate as it is in proportion to the plan and will reduce or enlarge accordingly.

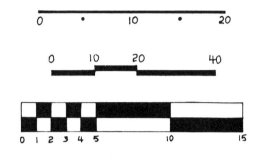

▲ Clients often find graphic scales easier to interpret than numerical scales.

Copyright

A further note regarding the copyright of the drawing can be shown as © Rosemary Alexander 1994. This clearly states that the copyright is the property of the designer and that the layout plan may not be copied without the express permission of the designer. Including this note can be a great help if clients ever mistakenly believe that they own the drawing.

Disclaimers

Including the disclaimer 'This drawing may not be scaled. All dimensions to be checked on site' is standard practice on many drawings. The term dates from times when plans were drawn on linen, which was prone to stretch and distort the plan. Nowadays, it simply means that although the layout plan has carefully been drawn to scale, the contractor is advised to check all dimensions on site before tendering or beginning construction, and it is used as a way of avoiding the responsibility for taking or transposing incorrect dimensions. This note should be set immediately above the title block.

Information panel

The width of the information panel should be in proportion to the sheet used and to the information to be included – say 100mm (4in) for an A2 (23½ × 16½in) sheet, and perhaps 125mm or 150mm (5–6in) for an A1 (33⅛ × 23½in) sheet. Notes on hard landscaping or plant lists will soon fill this space. The title block should sit in the bottom right-hand corner of the information panel and should be large enough to be readable if the drawing is later reduced in size.

Border

Borders are not essential, but having one will often enhance the look of a sheet. Once you have decided what type of border would be appropriate and where it should be located – 10mm (about ½in) from the edge of the sheet is usual – you can start to draw in the border in ink, using thick or thin lines. Alternatively, you can apply a zipper tone, which is available in many styles and thickness and is applied as a roll of adhesive tape. The right-hand side of the border can then become the outside line of the information panel.

▼ Examples of borders, which help to frame your sheet.

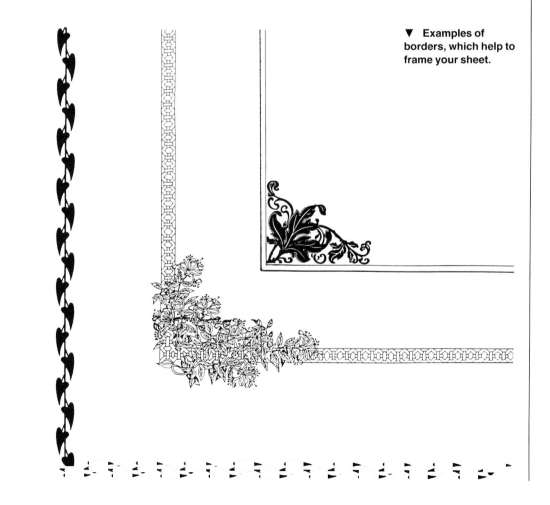

The plan and how to place it

The placing of the plan on the sheet determines how the finished garden layout plan will look. The entire sheet should be thought of as a piece of graphic design and be set out accordingly. Having designed the sheet layout, you must decide how best to arrange all the information that should be included.

First there will be the plan itself. At this stage it may be best to turn the sheet containing the site or base plan around to see how best it can be located on this fresh sheet, and to sketch out a dummy layout before beginning any drawing. The plan will need to be titled, and some of these titles may be extensive. Make sure that the sheet is large enough to accommodate all necessary infomation, because it will not be effective if data are squashed up or cramped.

Second, other items may need to be included – a section through the site, a detail of steps or an enticing bird's eye perspective, for example. Often these are drawn up separately, but this depends on the size of the sheet, the size of the garden, the scale at which it is drawn and how much back-up information you wish to show. The

size of these additional drawings should be carefully considered or, better still, completed in pencil and set up, rather like a collage, under your chosen sheet to see how much space they will take up before any final work is done.

If there is any danger of overcrowding, use a larger sheet, reduce the scale of the layout plan or put some information on a second sheet. The usual technique is to situate the main plan towards the bottom of the sheet, either in the centre or slightly to the left, and to arrange the

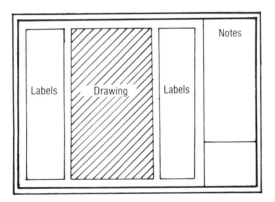

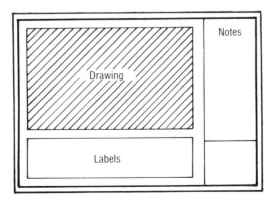

▲ The dimensions of your drawing will determine where you put labels.

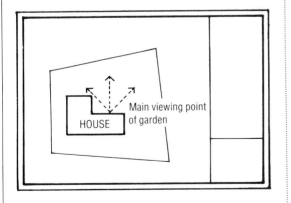

When positioning a plan consider from which direction the clients view their garden.

other information around it. All lines should begin at the same invisible margin, and here the graph paper backing sheet is an excellent guide. Care and time taken in thinking through or pasting up the sheet before actually inking in will save time and recriminations later.

North arrows

All garden layout or planting plans should include in the bottom right-hand corner adjacent to the title block an arrow or a north point indicating the northerly direction of the site. All that is required is an arrow and the letter N, but this can be shown in a variety of ways and be drawn with pen, stencils or dry transfers. Once a pleasing design has been worked out, it can be used for every drawing, with only the direction being adjusted, according to the site aspect. The north point, therefore, can be added to the tracing paper sheets only when the position of the plan has been decided.

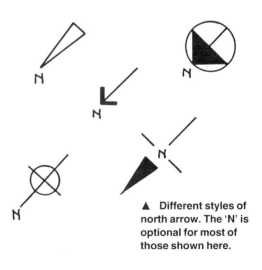

▲ Different styles of north arrow. The 'N' is optional for most of those shown here.

Once everything to be shown has been allocated a position, drawing up the final layout plan can begin, and should proceed quickly without too many changes or erasures.

8

The garden layout plan

The garden layout plan is the drawing from which the new garden will normally be set out and constructed, but before this can be undertaken, the plan must, of course, be approved by your client, who will want to see how it fulfils the brief you have been given.

The layout plan must be drawn accurately to scale so that everything shown on it can be reproduced in the garden. If your plan is drawn to a scale of 1 : 100 or even at 1 : 50 it may be too small to show in detail how you propose to construct such features as steps, walls or pergolas. These details can be shown on a separate drawing or detail sheet but if there is space around the plan, they may even be illustrated on the same sheet to help your client to interpret your ideas.

Before beginning to draw up your garden layout plans on your final sheet, it is useful to know the normal sequence that is followed.

Trace your final garden layout plan in ink or in pencil onto your final sheet (complete with title block and so forth) from your rough layout plan. This plan should show all areas of hard land-scaping as well as lawn and water within the site. Unless the site is very small, it will not usually include details of planting. Do not ink in over your pencil lines as the ink will not 'take', the graphite creating a barrier between the ink and the paper.

If, as is usual, you intend to create a separate planting plan, take a copy of your garden layout plan now, before you add in the labels, titling or any extra drawings. This copy, showing the hard landscaping with empty planting areas, can later be developed into the planting plan.

After taking a copy of your unlabelled garden layout plan, you can add any extra back-up drawings you may wish to have on this sheet, such as details, elevations and sections.

Once the drawings are all in place, you are ready to label the original. Many clients will ask you to do a garden layout plan first before they decide whether they want to commission a planting plan from you. To persuade them to do this, you may like to hint at your planting intentions on your garden layout plan, using appealing, descriptive phrases such as 'scented border to include lilacs, roses and lilies' or 'winter garden to include hellebores, bulbs and early-flowering shrubs'.

Pen nib sizes

Before you start to ink things in think about the nib sizes of the thicker nibs being used for the more dominant features. A variety of pen sizes gives enormous interest and relief to even the simplest drawing. Stencils and dry transfers can be used to label certain areas, such as house, garage or lawn, but use your own handwriting as much as possible – this saves your time and the client's money and gives a personal, informal touch to a drawing.

Enhancing your plan with shadow effects

As well as varying nib sizes to add depth to your plan, you can also apply shade and shadow effects, either to the original or to a copy for your client. Unless the shadows cast at various times of the day are a crucial aspect of your design, you need not worry about knowing exactly where they will fall throughout the day and at different times of the year. Your aim is to enhance the graphic quality of the plan and to make it more realistic and therefore easier for the client to understand.

Although the shadow casting need not be accurate, you can assume for the purposes of this exercise that the shadow will fall to the north side of all the objects in your plan and that the length of the shadow will be equal to the height of the object. Because you are using shadow for emphasis, you should use it selec-tively and resist the temptation to add it to everything. You may feel that on your garden layout plan you would like to emphasize the hard landscaping only and then, later, on your planting plan, the planting only. The choice is yours.

One rather subtle way of adding shadow to your original is by shading the back of the drawing with a soft pencil. You can then smudge the pencil with your finger to produce an even, soft effect. This will reproduce well by the dyeline process (see page 127), although the technique is rather less successful when it is photocopied.

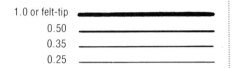

| 1.0 or felt-tip |
| 0.50 |
| 0.35 |
| 0.25 |

▶ **A variation of nib size or thickness of line makes the drawing easier to understand.**

▶ **Using shadow patterns on the shady side of plants makes a drawing more lifelike.**

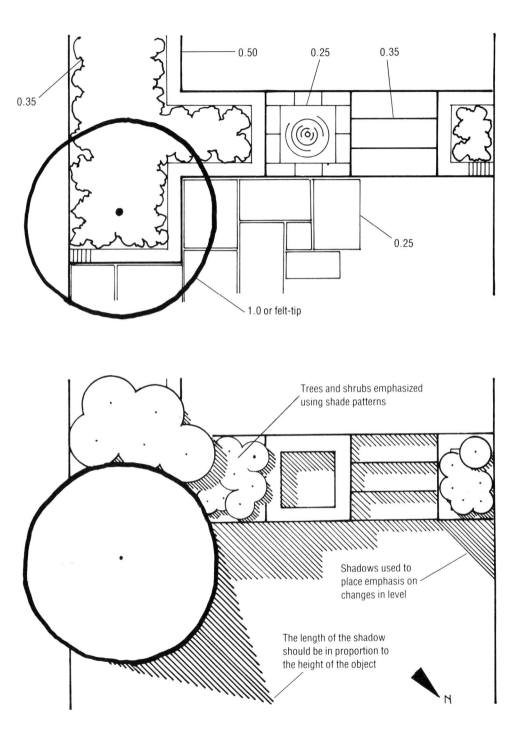

0.35

0.50   0.25   0.35

0.25

1.0 or felt-tip

Trees and shrubs emphasized using shade patterns

Shadows used to place emphasis on changes in level

The length of the shadow should be in proportion to the height of the object

N

Indicating different structures and surfaces

In drawing up the garden layout plan, it is usual first to locate the drawing centrally on the sheet, then to draw the house or any buildings in a heavy, continuous line, breaking it where doors and windows occur. In garden design, it is not usual to show the house wall as double thickness.

Boundaries

Boundaries are also drawn in at this stage. If they are marked by a free-standing wall this is usually shown as a double line of equal thickness, but if the boundaries are unfenced they are shown as a broken line.

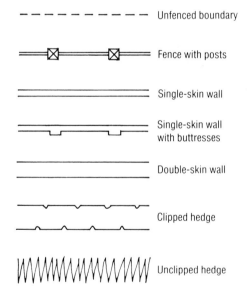

— — — — — — Unfenced boundary

Fence with posts

Single-skin wall

Single-skin wall with buttresses

Double-skin wall

Clipped hedge

Unclipped hedge

Doors The door is indicated by a single line at right angles to the wall, the swing of its opening edge being achieved by a semicircle. Occasionally, when the door lines at right angles may be confused with other lines on the drawing, they can be drawn at a lesser angle provided the same technique is used throughout the drawing.

Windows The representation of windows, differs according to whether they are of wood or metal, and they cannot be shown satisfactorily at less than 1 : 10. A single, finer line should be used.

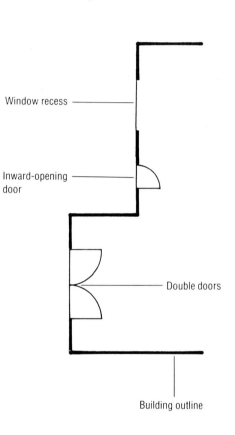

Window recess

Inward-opening door

Double doors

Building outline

Terraces or paved areas

Where possible, the material used for a terrace or paved area should be in keeping with the house and the locality – a combination of stone and brick, perhaps, or stone with a brick surround. If the budget is tight, gravel may be a cheaper alternative. Depending on your scale, gravel can be indicated by tiny circles interspersed with dots or simply by dots.

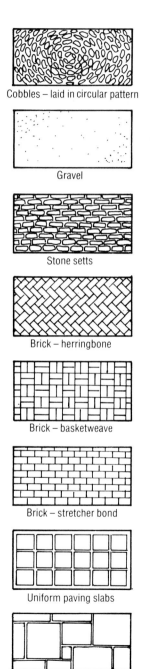

Cobbles – laid in circular pattern

Gravel

Stone setts

Brick – herringbone

Brick – basketweave

Brick – stretcher bond

Uniform paving slabs

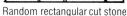
Random rectangular cut stone

Paths

Paths can be of many different materials – stone, brick, concrete or gravel – but they should also be in keeping with the architecture. They can be illustrated, to show the material and, in the case of brick or other paving, the directional flow. Any edgings, such as brick, or a timber strip to separate gravel and borders or grass, must also be indicated. Remember that when they are seen from above, every object on the plan should be clearly defined and even in the case of narrow or thin edgings, both sides must be shown by two lines.

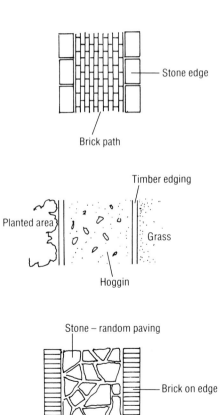

Stone edge

Brick path

Timber edging

Planted area

Grass

Hoggin

Stone – random paving

Brick on edge

Steps

Steps should be drawn to show the desired number of treads and the width of each. Arrows should always point upwards, with the line of the arrow beginning at the outer edge of the first riser. Often the word 'up' will be included, and for clarity risers may be numbered in order, beginning with the lowest, the first riser being shown by a dot on the line of the arrow. If the steps are flanked by a railing or retaining wall, this must also be shown. The height of each riser, which cannot be shown on a flat plan, can be stated either by titling or as a note in the information panel.

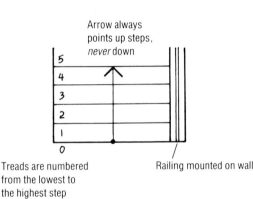

Arrow always points up steps, *never* down

Treads are numbered from the lowest to the highest step

Railing mounted on wall

Ramps

Should have an arrow pointing in the 'up' direction and should be titled as 'ramp'. The angle of rise – 15° maximum – should be shown on a section (see Chapter 9).

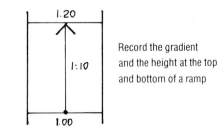

1.20

1:10

1.00

Record the gradient and the height at the top and bottom of a ramp

Walls

Both retaining and free-standing walls can be of various heights. A low retaining wall of four or five brick courses can double as an extra seating area, while higher, free-standing walls may need expansion joints and buttresses to support them.

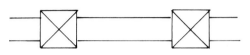

Concrete block wall with concrete-capped piers

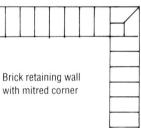

Brick retaining wall with mitred corner

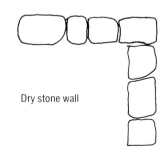

Dry stone wall

There are even such curiosities as wavy or crinkle-crankle walls, and although these are expensive to build, they are reputed to be very sturdy.

The final course or coping of a wall has a crucial effect on its appearance, and it needs to be thought through carefully. Both coping and the bond must be shown in an elevation or detail, or labelled. If the corners of the wall are to be finished off in a particular way, this, too, should be shown. The height of the wall can be written in or included in your notes. Fences are shown as a double line, while small rectangles indicate the upright fence posts.

Ponds and areas of water
To indicate a still stretch of water, draw broken lines to simulate light shining on water. A fountain can be shown as a small circle with other circles representing ripples emanating from it. In both cases, titling will help to clarify the meaning.

Still water

Water with fountain

Pergolas and other ornamental features
Both vertical and horizontal dimensions of ornamental features should be shown, and because the drawing is to scale, the size at which they are drawn will depend on the material used – stone, brick, timber or metal. Arches are indicated in the same way as pergolas. If plants are being drawn to cover them, they can also be shown, provided they do not confuse the drawing.

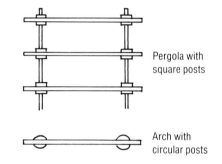

Pergola with square posts

Arch with circular posts

Statues, urns and pots
Statues or urns usually have to stand on plinths, which should be in proportion with whatever stands on them. Fixing details must ensure safety, and here again advice can be sought. They are usually shown as circles on a square base, or simply as a circle within a circle drawn with a circle template, to indicate the inner and outer thickness of the object. Planting within may be shown if wished.

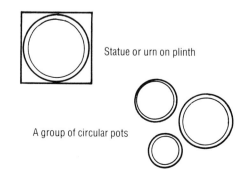

Statue or urn on plinth

A group of circular pots

Ground shaping or slopes
Contours are shown as a broken line, with existing contours having longer dashes than proposed contours. Their height, which should be related to a datum height or level, can be written beside the lines. The closer the contours, the steeper the gradient. Slopes or embankments can be shown as Vs or as arrows pointing downwards, and their proximity will again indicate the gradient.

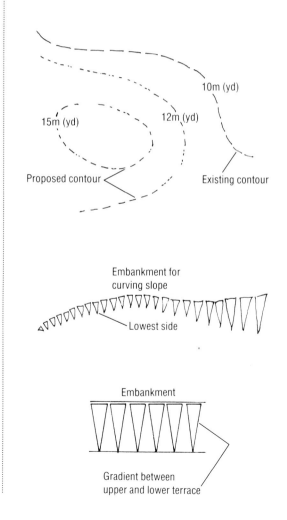

10m (yd)

15m (yd)

12m (yd)

Proposed contour

Existing contour

Embankment for curving slope

Lowest side

Embankment

Gradient between upper and lower terrace

Drainage, irrigation and electricity

Drainage, irrigation and electricity must also be incorporated at the design stage, because work may need to be carried out before the main construction begins, and each arrangement will vary according to the site limitations. These hidden costs can soon mount up, and they must, therefore, be included in the written specification to the contractor that should accompany the design.

Sometimes it is necessary to indicate the junction of drains at the downpipes of the house, and this is done with a small circle and appropriate letters. Gullies are shown as a square, and a crossfall to them is indicated with a small arrow. Manhole covers are shown as a bisected rectangle and the letters MH.

Irrigation is simply shown as a broken line, and the position of any sprinklers in a lawn, for instance, can be marked with a small cross and titled.

Electricity cables are also indicated with a broken line.

Irrigation and electric cables and lighting points should be titled to avoid confusion. Wall sockets are normally indicated as a half circle.

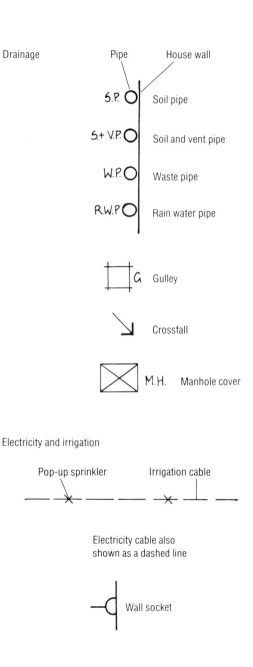

Drainage

S.P. ◯ Soil pipe

S.+V.P. ◯ Soil and vent pipe

W.P. ◯ Waste pipe

R.W.P ◯ Rain water pipe

G Gulley

Crossfall

M.H. Manhole cover

Electricity and irrigation

Pop-up sprinkler   Irrigation cable

Electricity cable also shown as a dashed line

Wall socket

Alterations or additions

A clear distinction must be made between existing and proposed work, with only the minimum essential outlines of the former being drawn, the new work being indicated in the usual manner. Proposed walls are usually shown as outlines in a heavy black line, and existing walls are drawn in a finer line or in pencil.

Communication is the main objective in presenting a garden layout plan to a client, and the plan should, therefore, look as realistic as possible. There are really no set rules for symbols of garden structures, but whatever is shown must be drawn to scale. It can be difficult to draw a realistic brick path to a scale of 1 : 100 or even at 1 : 50, and the average client would probably prefer a smaller bill than to see every brick carefully illustrated.

In order to explain what is envisaged, a small, more detailed sketch, at a scale of 1 : 5, 1 : 10 or 1 : 20, can accompany the layout plan to give a clear idea of the intentions. The symbols should be drawn in different thicknesses of line depending on the dominance of the feature – houses and trees will be indicated in a heavier line than pots, brick edging or ground-cover planting, for example. Many designers spend too much time on elaborate graphics. Clear, simple plans are less time consuming to produce and, therefore, less expensive for the client.

9

Sections and elevations

Although the garden layout plan has been completed, many clients cannot understand or visualize a flat plan, and some additional explanatory drawings may be necessary. The contractor or garden builder may also require further drawings to clarify the overall concept and, although spot heights and levels should be included, a section or sections taken through the garden will make the various heights and levels understood.

Sections, elevations and section-elevations are all used to show the detail of vertical elements in the garden, whether it is the whole garden that needs to be shown or details of a specific item, such as a pond, for construction purposes.

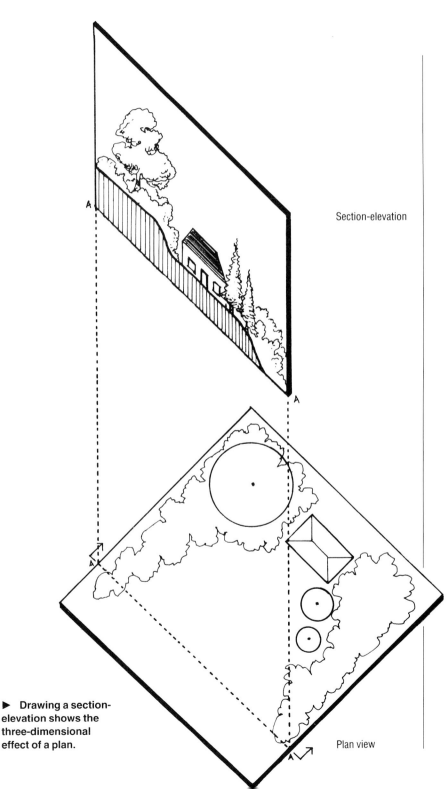

Section-elevation

▶ Drawing a section-elevation shows the three-dimensional effect of a plan.

Plan view

Sections In a true section no surface details are shown, only the outlined shapes of elements along the cut line are included; these may be useful for showing changes of level and for some construction drawings.

Elevations, on the other hand, do show surface details, as well as elements beyond and, sometimes, just before the cut line, although in an elevation the cut line itself is not shown. Architects often use elevations to show details of house façades, and they can be useful for showing planting areas.

Section-elevations are, as their name suggests, a combination of sections and elevations. They are often referred to as landscape sections or simply sections, although they are not true sections, showing both a prominent cut line and surface details of vertical features on and beyond the cut line. Section-elevations are quick and easy to draw because all the vertical objects shown are drawn at their proper scale, no matter how far they are from the cut line.

Section

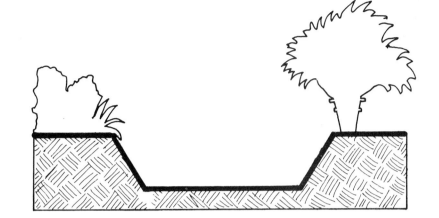

Elevation

Section-elevation

Normally, two sections are sufficient for the small or average sized garden, but if there are several changes of level or if the garden is large, more may be necessary. Usually, the first section is taken through the entire length of the garden, and the second section is taken across the width of the garden. In each case the exact beginning and end should be clearly indicated on both the plan and the sectional drawing. For example, the first section may be extended from the house wall to the distant boundary and may include only the terrace, lawn and some planting, while the second section may run from the boundary wall to the opposite boundary wall, but will include a greenhouse, steps, arch, tree or anything else that occurs on the section line shown. There is no standard point at which a section should be taken, but it is sensible to carry the line through at a point where there are various changes in level, both above and below ground level, or where there is a certain amount of vertical interest to be explained.

Enlarging the scale

If the plan is drawn to a scale of 1 : 100 or smaller, it may be difficult to show in sufficient detail what is going on unless the proposed garden is on a steep slope that is being transformed into a series of terraces. If necessary, the section can be drawn in a larger scale, say to 1 : 50 or even 1 : 20. Occasionally, the horizontal scale may remain at 1 : 100, while the vertical scale is shown at 1 : 50, but this can be rather distorting and should be used only for showing reshaped landforms, but not for the average small garden.

It is as important to show what goes on below ground level as to show what happens above. This may be a swimming pool, pond, sunken terrace, structural foundations of walls, hedges, tree pits or existing tree roots.

If, at each side of the section, the overall height is also indicated to scale, there can be no misunderstanding. It also helps to relate the proposals to surrounding buildings. Sometimes it is useful to include with the section a drawn-to-scale human figure, perhaps standing under the pergola, so that the client may identify with the scale.

Groundworks or contouring

Sections are also necessary where major groundworks occur or where there is re-contouring or 'cut and fill'. The existing land formation level can be shown in one way and the proposed levels in another, with key spot heights always being indicated as on the layout plan. This may help the client to understand the proposal and to assist in calculations for moving or importing soil on the site. It is possible that you have overlooked the need for access for earth-moving equipment or the removal of unwanted soil, and the removal and reconstruction of a gateway or part of a wall to allow vehicular access will be an additional and perhaps unforeseen expense.

Where to place sections on a sheet

These sections can either be drawn on a separate sheet or, if there is space, they can be included on the same sheet as the layout plan. Place the section in an easily identifiable position so that its relationship to the layout plan is obvious. This may mean having one section running horizontally across the sheet and the other running vertically, or both sections running horizontally. Choose whatever is clear and looks effective, while at the same time making sure that any figures or writing can be easily read without the reader having to twist his or her head sideways. Because it is larger, the layout plan is usually best placed lower on the sheet, with a section or sections shown above it, and the name and location of the section being indicated on the plan, with arrows indicating the direction from which they have been drawn.

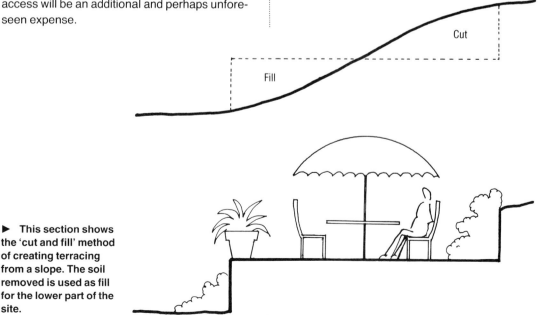

▶ **This section shows the 'cut and fill' method of creating terracing from a slope. The soil removed is used as fill for the lower part of the site.**

Detailed drawings

Depending on the subject being shown and the complexity of the detail to be shown, these drawings can be at a scale of 1 : 50 down to 1 : 20, 1 : 10, or even at 1 : 1. As they may be interpreted as actual construction drawings, it is unwise to include such detailed drawings unless you are completely familiar with or knowledge-able about how to build them. Unless you are a qualified architect, landscape architect or surveyor, it may be wiser to show the contractor a rough sketch, photograph or a real-life example of what you intend, because the client could take legal action against you should the construction detail prove faulty.

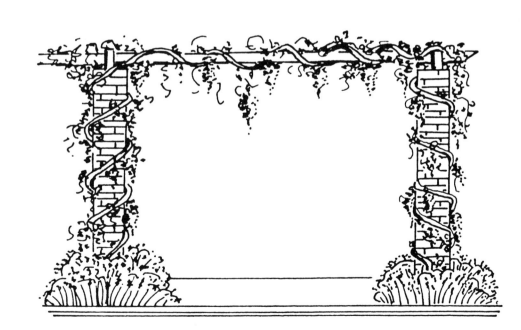

Examples of detail drawings, drawn to scale.

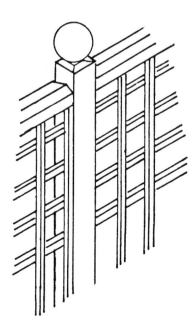

75

Construction details

It is frequently impossible to show on garden layout plans the detailed proposals for the construction of paths, paving, steps, arches or other hard landscaping items. In the construction of roof terraces, where there may be a heavy weight load for instance, it may be necessary to show each layer of material, hard and soft, to make the method of building absolutely clear.

Certain areas might need to be drawn in greater detail, showing the internal structure of all the components and how they fit together. These drawings are again largely sectional, and they should be drawn to scale, indicating the materials used, and their dimension and thickness shown with strong pen or pencil lines, the written dimensions also being included to avoid misinterpretation.

Construction details are not usually drawn on the same sheet as the garden plan but on a separate sheet or sheets of tracing paper, which are normally given to the builder or engineer. Occasionally a designer may plan the garden layout, but may then seek the advice of or enlist the services of an architect, architectural technician or other professional to carry out the detailed construction drawing, particularly if these are to be classed as working drawings, from which the subject will be built.

If the main purpose of your detailed drawings is to help communicate ideas to your client, you may wish to position them around the garden layout plan. This may not be an approved standard practice and can be confusing, but if there is space on the sheet, it may be aesthetically pleasing and help to sell the concept.

▶ **Simple construction sections, drawn to scale, can be filed and reused, with minor modifications, on many different projects.**

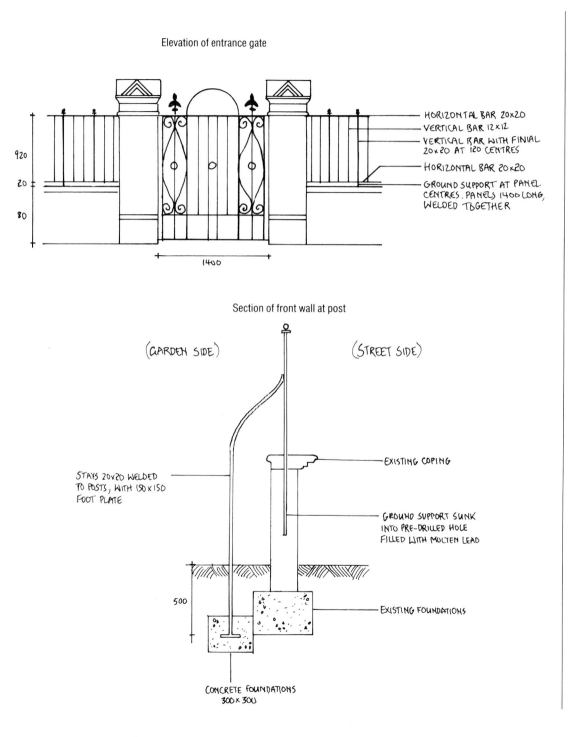

Elevation of entrance gate

HORIZONTAL BAR 20×20
VERTICAL BAR 12×12
VERTICAL BAR WITH FINIAL 20×20 AT 120 CENTRES
HORIZONTAL BAR 20×20
GROUND SUPPORT AT PANEL CENTRES. PANELS 1400 LONG, WELDED TOGETHER

920
20
80
1400

Section of front wall at post

(GARDEN SIDE)   (STREET SIDE)

STAYS 20×20 WELDED TO POSTS, WITH 150×150 FOOT PLATE

EXISTING COPING

GROUND SUPPORT SUNK INTO PRE-DRILLED HOLE FILLED WITH MOLTEN LEAD

EXISTING FOUNDATIONS

500

CONCRETE FOUNDATIONS 300×300

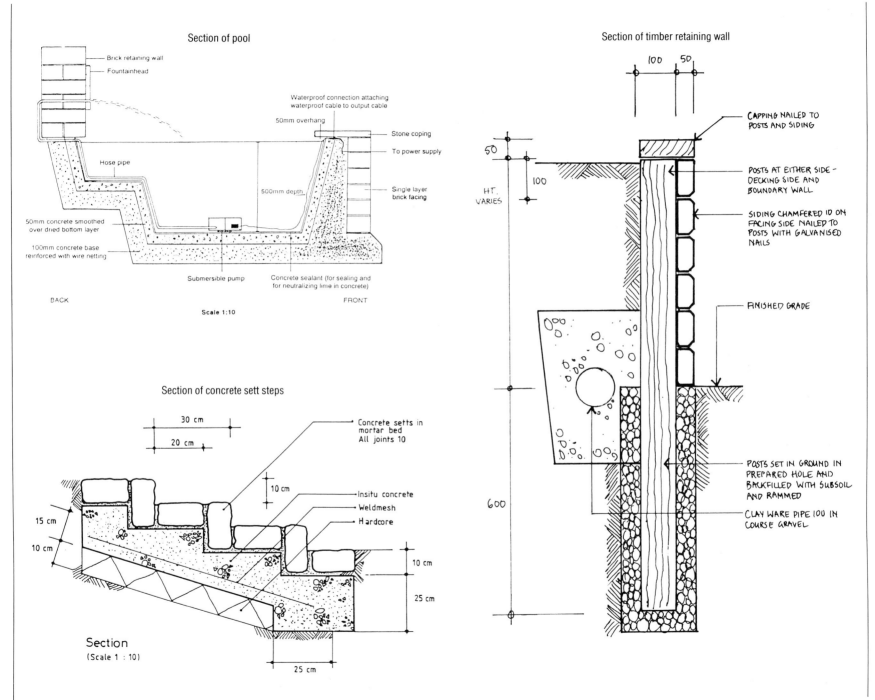

Section of pool

Brick retaining wall
Fountainhead

Waterproof connection attaching
waterproof cable to output cable

50mm overhang

Stone coping

To power supply

Hose pipe

Single layer
brick facing

500mm depth

50mm concrete smoothed
over dried bottom layer

100mm concrete base
reinforced with wire netting

Submersible pump

Concrete sealant (for sealing and
for neutralizing lime in concrete)

BACK

FRONT

Scale 1:10

Section of concrete sett steps

30 cm

20 cm

Concrete setts in
mortar bed
All joints 10

10 cm

Insitu concrete

Weldmesh

Hardcore

15 cm

10 cm

10 cm

25 cm

Section
(Scale 1 : 10)

25 cm

Section of timber retaining wall

100   50

CAPPING NAILED TO
POSTS AND SIDING

50

100

HT.
VARIES

POSTS AT EITHER SIDE -
DECKING SIDE AND
BOUNDARY WALL

SIDING CHAMFERED 10 ON
FACING SIDE NAILED TO
POSTS WITH GALVANISED
NAILS

FINISHED GRADE

600

POSTS SET IN GROUND IN
PREPARED HOLE AND
BACKFILLED WITH SUBSOIL
AND RAMMED

CLAY WARE PIPE 100 IN
COURSE GRAVEL

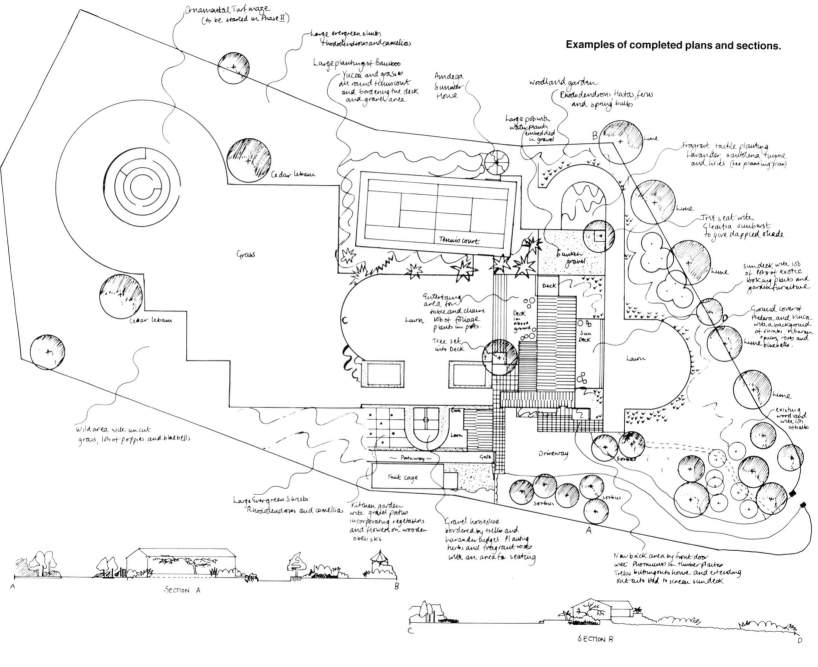

Examples of completed plans and sections.

Ornamental Turf maze
(to be started in Phase II)

Large evergreen shrubs
rhododendrons and camellias

Large planting of Bamboo
Yucca and grasses
all round tennis court
and bordering the deck
and gravel area.

Amdega Summer House

Woodland garden
Rhododendrons, Hostas, ferns
and spring bulbs

Large pots with
water plants
embedded
in gravel

B

Lime

Fragrant tactile planting
Lavander, santolina thyme
and lilies (see planting plan)

Cedar lebani

Lime

Tree seat with
Gleditsia sunburst
to give dappled shade.

Tennis court

Sunken gravel

Deck

Lime

sun deck with lots
of pots of exotic
looking plants and
garden furniture

Grass

Entertaining
area for
table and chairs
lots of foliage
plants in pots.

Deck in above
ground

Sun Deck

Lawn

Ground cover of
Hedera and vinca
with a background
of shrubs viburnum
opulus roots and
lime bluebells.

Lawn

Cedar lebani

Tree set
into Deck.

Lawn

Lime

existing
woodland
with lots
of bulbs

Wild area with uncut
grass, lots of poppies and bluebells

Gate

Lawn

Gate

Driveway

Sorbus

Pathway

Fruit cage

Large evergreen shrubs.
Rhododendrons and camellias

Kitchen garden
with gravel paths
incorporating vegetables
and flowers on wooden
obelisks

Gravel horseshoe
bordered by trellis and
lavander hedges. Planting
herbs and fragrant roses
with an area for seating

Sorbus

Sorbus

A

New brick area by front door
with Phormiums in timber planter
Trellis butting onto house and extending
out into bed to screen sundeck

Section A

A

B

Section B

C

D

▲ A continental approach has been adopted for this country garden. To make full use of the space, the garden has been divided into a series of rooms connected by walkways, with extensive timber decking around the house providing areas for sitting and for entertaining.

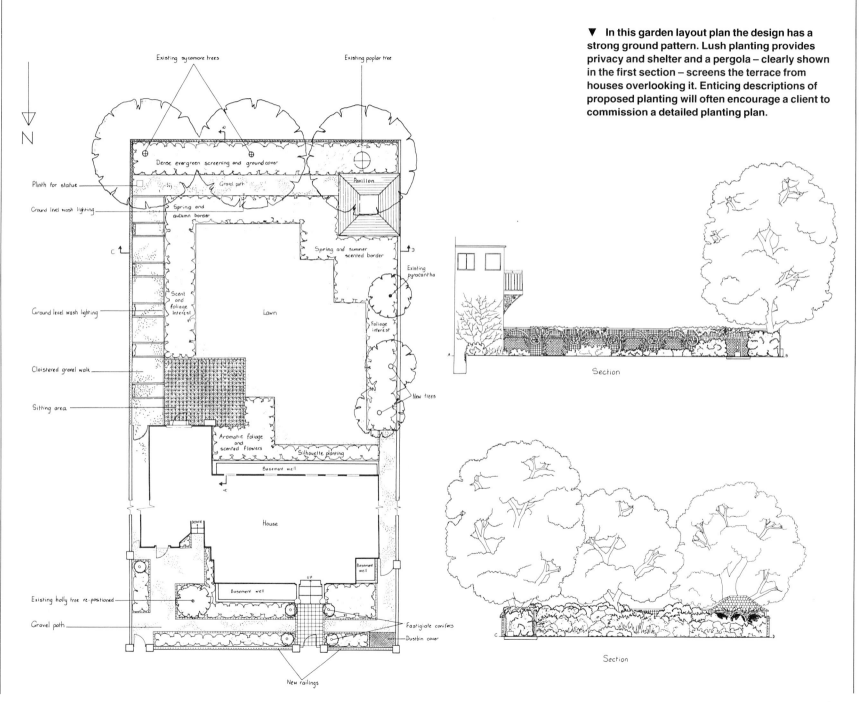

N

Existing sycamore trees

Existing poplar tree

Dense evergreen screening and ground cover

Plinth for statue

Ground level wash lighting

Gravel path

Pavilion

Spring and autumn border

Spring and summer scented border

C

D

Existing pyracantha

Scent and foliage interest

Ground level wash lighting

Lawn

Foliage interest

Cloistered gravel walk

Sitting area

New trees

Aromatic foliage and scented flowers

Silhouette planting

Basement well

A

House

DOWN

Basement well

Existing holly tree re-positioned

Basement well

Gravel path

UP

Fastigiate conifers

Dustbin cover

New railings

▼ In this garden layout plan the design has a strong ground pattern. Lush planting provides privacy and shelter and a pergola – clearly shown in the first section – screens the terrace from houses overlooking it. Enticing descriptions of proposed planting will often encourage a client to commission a detailed planting plan.

A   B

Section

C   D

Section

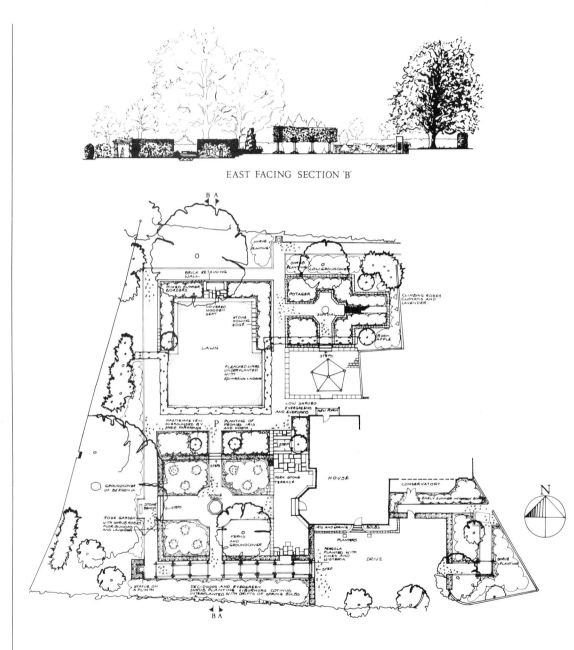

EAST FACING SECTION 'B'

▲ The brief for this site was to design an intimate, secluded, yet formal garden. The space has been divided to create a series of distinct, symmetrical areas linked by hedges.

Standard symbols

There may be no standard way of indicating materials on a layout plan, but in sections or elevations there are accepted standard methods, and these must be followed so that the different materials can be easily distinguished. There are conventional ways of indicating materials in general use, in which all lines or hatching are drawn diagonally at 45°, the spacing of the lines varying according to the scale of the drawing, but the general proportions being followed. Where large areas of cross-hatching need to be shown, it is only necessary to indicate a portion near the edge or ends, the hatching gradually being faded out towards the middle. If there is any possibility that the symbols used on any of your plans are likely to cause confusion, a legend or key may be drawn in the right-hand information panel.

Abbreviations of words

There is an accepted conventional standard in the abbreviation of words commonly used on drawings, and using these also helps to avoid confusion. Although it is unlikely that all of these will be used in a garden design, familiarity with them may help you decipher other drawings.

Materials and general terms

Aggregate	Agg
Approved	appd
Approximate	approx
Asbestos	Asb
Asphalt	Asph
Bench mark	BM
Bitumen	Bitn
Brickwork	Bwk *or* B
British Standard	BS
Cast iron	CI
Cement	Cem
Centre line	CL *or* C
Centre to centre	c/c
Concrete	Conc

Diameter	dia
Drawing	Dwg
Galvanized	Galv
Ground level	GL
Gully	G
Height	ht
Insulated *or* insulation	insul
Invert	inv
Left hand	LH
Macadam	MAC
Manhole	MH
Not to scale	NTS
Number	No
Radius	rad
Rain-water pipe	RWP
Reinforced concrete	RC
Rain-water outlet	RWO
Round	rd
Sketch	sk
Soil and vent pipe	S&VP
Soil pipe	SP
Specification	Spec
Square	sq
Standard Wire Gauge	SWG
Stand pipe	St P
Street gully	SG
Tongued and grooved	T&G
Traced	Tcd
Volume	vol
Waste pipe	WP
Waste and vent pipe	W&VP
Water closet	WC

Indicating materials on vertical constructions

The following are the accepted ways of indicating materials in sections.

Brickwork
At scales of 1 : 100 and less, brickwork is indicated in section by two solid 45° diagonal lines drawn close together. It is easiest to draw in the diagonal lines by setting out the heights of the courses on a vertical line at the left-hand side of the sheet and then draw them by using a 45° set-square balanced against your T-square or parallel motion.

Stonework
Stone walls are indicated in section as solid black at 1 : 100 and smaller scales. When they are drawn at a larger scale – 1 : 50 or 1 : 20 – the individual stones can be shown.

Timber
Continuous thin lines at the appropriate scale are used to represent vertical or horizontal timber in section at scales of 1 : 50 and less.

Reinforced concrete
This can be shown in the conventional representation in various scales.

Brickwork (at 1:20)

Brickwork (at 1:50)

Brickwork (at 1:100)

Brickwork (at scales of over 1:100)

Cement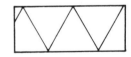

Soil

Note that soil is usually hatched freehand

Hardcore

Concrete

Show the aggregate in small areas

Timber

Masonry

▶ **Conventional methods of representing materials on sectional drawings.**

10

The planting plan

All garden designers have their own particular method of working up a planting plan, and it is unlikely that any two designers would approach or carry through their planting design in the same way. The most important thing is to find a simple, and therefore relatively quick, method of showing the interplay between plants – not only for a client, but also for you, as the designer, to check that there is sufficient contrast or balance of form, texture and colour in the proposed planting.

What to aim for

Some designers who may have a very clear idea of the desired effect do a quick outline elevation before beginning their planting plan and find it easier to work from this, backwards, as it were, to the flat plan. Other designers, faced with an empty planting area, immediately begin thinking about what each plant will be and give the full botanical name to each circle or outline shape as they work up the plan. There are no hard and fast rules – simply experiment until you find a method that suits you.

Speed is important because you will charge your client for your time.

As with most designers, your particular graphic style will develop with practice. Experiment with different techniques, try to see the work of other designers and look at how they present their planting plans. Are their plans sufficiently straightforward for a 'non-visual' client to understand? Would they be easy to plant from?

Working up a planting plan is often the most testing part of a garden designer's work. The expertise lies in selecting, grouping together and using plants to achieve certain requirements, such as dramatic foliage in a narrow, dry border, or using pale shades to lighten a dark, shady area. Although the individual plants must be able to cope with the constraints of the site, it is the grouping or massed effect of the planting that will provide the visual interest.

Most clients are not interested in obscure plants. The usual requests are for year-round interest, colour and low maintenance. Your planting plan should indicate the positions of all trees and shrubs, herbaceous or ground-cover plants, bulbs and annuals, and it should also state how many of each are required. As the plan will be used not just as a basis for ordering the plants but for allocating their planting positions after delivery, it must be accurate and easy to understand. A planting plan on paper also helps to produce a better composed and more balanced effect and will also serve as a record of what has been planted.

Developing a detailed planting plan usually follows the acceptance of the layout plan by the client. There is absolutely no point in wasting your time and the client's money in producing a detailed planting plan until the garden layout has been decided. In preparing your layout plan, you may have made decisions about the planting that ought to be adhered to – for example, 'scented border' or 'shady border to include ferns and bulbs' – and you may, for instance, have committed yourself to using certain types of plants or to including a particular tree or shrub in a border. Clients will often require you to work with existing plants or structures.

As you draw up the planting plan, remember that it is also the designer's responsibility to reject any plants that are substitutes, substandard or incorrectly labelled. This is difficult to do if you are unfamiliar with the plant and have only recently made its acquaintance through a catalogue or book!

Points to consider before plant selection

Before you rush into plant selection, there are many points that you should consider. First, reflect on the hard materials used in the layout plan and the period and architectural style of any buildings. The types of plants used should complement these. The size or proportion of the buildings and the space to be planted will affect both the choice of plants and the groupings – you may need strong outline shapes and large groups of a single type of plant to link a large mass of building with planting. Aspect, micro-climate, soil conditions, site constraints, the client's lifestyle and preferences, colour palette, seasonal effects and budget will all affect your choice, and it is useful to refer back to your site analysis and report to remind yourself of any limitations.

Quality of light

Think of the quality of light and how it will affect your planting. The latitude will affect the intensity of the light, and shadow patterns and outlines shapes are more clearly defined in some areas, while in others only strong foreground shapes may stand out. Gertrude Jekyll, one of Britain's most brilliant garden designers, already had poor eyesight when she began drawing garden plans, and she relied heavily on outline shape for her excellent plant groupings.

Suitable varieties

The plants you choose ought to be in proportion to their surroundings. Delicate leaf shapes and fragile flowers will look out of place if they have to compete for attention with a modern tower block. The distinctive outline shape of the plants and their form, texture and scent will make your planting groupings memorable and are usually more important than comparatively fleeting flowers.

You should also consider the ecological relation-ship of the plants. Lavender and rhododendrons will not only look unnatural together, but they require different soil conditions. Keep a plant notebook, and when you visit gardens, write down not only the plants that you like, but also note the companion planting. The effect may be made in the way the plants are grouped, not in the individual plant. Referring back to these plant notebooks may provide you with inspiration when time is short and your imagination is at a standstill.

When you name plants, always use the most up-to-date botanical name, because common names vary widely from country to country.

Form and texture

The shape or form of a plant and its leaf colour and texture, rather than the flowers, should be the main consideration when choosing plants. This will give contrast and long-lasting visual interest to your designs. Round plants should be interspersed with spiky or tiered shapes, such as yucca or *Viburnum plicatum*, which will relieve a regimented, 'bun' like outline. Try to think of the leaf colour and texture as fabric, contrasting a glossy satin finish, such as aucuba, with the more matt, velvety leaves of, say, verbascum.

Light reflection and absorption

Do not overlook the light reflective or light-absorbent qualities of the leaves. Glossy evergreens, such as *Choisya ternata* or *Aucuba japonica*, reflect the light, while yew (*Taxus*) absorbs it. Using light-reflective and absorbent material or introducing silver (*Convolvulus cneorum*) or blue-green foliage (*Euphorbia wulfenii*) into a border can maintain interest without anything being in flower.

Scent

The scent of flowers is one of the great pleasures of a garden. Try not only to choose a fragrant species, but also to think about the time of day that the plant gives off the perfume. Some plants, such as nicotiana, are heavily scented in the evening, to attract moths, while others, such as *Viburnum carlesii*, can be enjoyed throughout the day. It is often assumed that all roses or honeysuckles will have a perfume, and how disappointing it can be to a client to discover that the particular variety chosen by you does not have this particular attribute.

Colour

This can be a very emotive subject. Almost every client has a particular dislike – mauve or orange, perhaps – but will be less definite about what they do like. The request for 'lots of colour' is often misleading, and you should always consider the interior colour scheme and try to reflect it in the garden. Entire beds or garden rooms can be planted in blends or contrasts, while an indiscriminate mixture of colour is as jarring to the eye in a garden as it would be in a room or on a person.

Blends of colours A scheme in which blends of colour, such as creams moving through yellows to apricot or orange, perhaps highlighted by blue, or by a planting of pale pinks to reds to mauves, can be successful provided that they are appropriate to their surroundings. A bed of pink flowers backed by a red brick wall could look horrific, while the same flowers might be a marvellous contrast to a light-absorbent yew hedge. Foliage borders, too, can concentrate on blends of a single hue – yellows lighting up a dark corner or silvers giving a cooling effect.

Contrasting colours A blue-tinged, northern light shows off to advantage the soft pinks, blues and silvers that are popular in so many gardens. Clashes of stronger colours, such as orange and purple, are less familiar but can, if used with discretion, be equally effective and less predictable. So much depends on the backdrop.

Sometimes colours follow the current fashion, with perhaps pink flowers backed with green foliage picking up the latest fad from the fashion houses. Clear blues, yellows and reds tend to brighten overcast spring days, and in autumn the more fiery, reddish tints of leaves, contrasting with the purplish-blue of Michaelmas daisies, are effective in crisp, cooler weather.

Single colours A garden or garden room that concentrates on a single colour, such as white, can be very striking. It is possible to use not only white flowers, but white-veined or marbled leaves such as *Eryngium bourgatii* 'Oxford Blue', the felted grey-leaved *Stachys byzantina* offset by glossy green foliage, such as the hart's tongue fern (*Phylittis scolopendrium*), can be exciting both for designer and client. There are many other single-colour possibilities, but in all cases a selection of matching and contrasting foliage is needed to carry through and soften the idea.

Other limiting factors
There will be many functional reasons for plant choice, but this will vary with every site, and you should refer back to the site analysis and, if available, your report as *aide-mémoires*. The functional considerations could be the need to screen or frame views, provide shade, filter wind or noise or direct circulation.

Reference books and catalogues
Most designers quickly accumulate a library of reference books and catalogues, and you will probably already have some reliable favourites ready to consult. Often, much valuable design time is taken up searching for inspiration, and a more disciplined approach can be to develop the planting plan by looking at the composition of two-dimensional forms on the ground plane, by quickly sketching the horizontal relationship

between the proposed plants and their surroundings, and then to build on these to provide the complete spatial plan in three dimensions. These quick sketches can help you to visualize your groupings within their setting, before you consult books or catalogues, to which you can refer only to confirm plants' suitability and, possibly, spelling.

No two books will agree totally on plant behaviour and characteristics, and there is no substitute for a sound personal knowledge of the plants you have selected. Try not to be too ambitious and, at least to begin with, use popular plants whose attributes and performance have made them well known.

If possible, all plants should be obtained from one reliable stockist, often a wholesale or retail nursery. Garden centres tend to be expensive and are usually less willing to give a discount for bulk orders.

Suppliers
Use only the catalogue of those nurseries from which you intend to order plants. Obtaining plants from too many sources is not only time-consuming and therefore expensive, but it also means that the plants may be delivered at different times. It is much easier to execute a planting plan on site if you have your entire palette of plants at your disposal, rather than having to leave gaps for late arrivals.

For your embryonic or evolving plan try not to use a catalogue, but think only of outline shapes and textures. Only when your plant positions are on the plan and you have established an overall feeling for what you are trying to achieve, should you actually put names to the plants. If you use a catalogue from the beginning, you will have filled up your planting plan before you reach the middle of the alphabet.

Key and skeleton plants
Some key and skeleton plants will be needed to link the planting to the buildings or surrounding landscape. The key plant should have some quality that makes it stand out as a feature from the rest of the planting. This may be the outline form, as with phormium, the foliage shape of a plant such as fatsia, or simply its colour, as with *Robinia pseudoacacia* 'Frisia'. A distinctive tree or large shrub can act as a pivot round which the rest of the planting revolves. Although you are working on a flat plan, you need to visualize not only the dimensions of the plants but also their outline shapes and textures.

With the key plants in place you can choose the skeleton plants, those that have a good, year-round outline shape, and here texture will offset the more ephemeral planting.

After your key and skeleton plants are in place, the flowering shrubs may be chosen, although often the best plants are those whose flowers are shown off by their foliage, such as a pink rose with glaucous blue leaves, or a white cistus with glossy green leaves. Try to vary the outline shapes by including plants with spiky, rounded or layered silhouettes.

Climbers and wall shrubs
These are useful not only for softening structures but also because they can quickly add a third dimension to borders, particularly narrow ones at the base of a house wall. Deciduous border planting can be set off by a backdrop of evergreen *Clematis armandii* or *Hedera* (ivy) or a blue and yellow colour scheme can be accentuated by the rambling rose 'Goldfinch' and blue *Ceanothus impressus*.

Herbaceous or ground-cover plants
These plants can be used to soften the overall effect as well as reducing maintenance. Large-

leaved plants, such as bergenias or hostas, can contrast with the more delicate foliage of thalictrum, while the woolly, grey foliage of *Stachys byzantina* or a spreading carpet of *Ajuga reptans* may be effective creeping through other plants at the front of a border.

Bamboos, ferns and grasses

Although they can be invasive, bamboos can give an oriental flavour and the taller varieties can be effective for screening. The inclusion of grasses or ferns tends to give a more natural look. Strictly speaking, they should be classed separately on a plant list, but are often included with other categories.

Infill plants

Particularly helpful for bulking up a newly planted garden, infill plants can be used temporarily among the permanent planting until it has matured.

Annuals such as *Nicotiana sylvestris* or clumps of forget-me-nots, which self-seed if allowed, can help to cover the soil in the early stages, while cuttings can be taken from the more tender species, such as osteospermum, overwintered in the greenhouse and used again the following year.

Bulbs, corms and rhizomes

These not only maximize the use of the soil by being planted under other plants, but they can enliven the borders early in the year and may extend the flowering season throughout the summer and early autumn. Smaller bulbs such as *Tritelia laxa* can help carry through a blue scheme, while the taller, scented *Lilium regale* can give a paler effect amongst larger plantings.

Starting the planting plan

Using your garden layout plan as an underlay, lay a sheet of tracing paper over it and trace off the proposed planting areas. These areas can either remain at their original scale, or they can be enlarged to any desired scale – 1 : 50 or 1 : 100 is usually preferred – but if the site is very large you may wish to show the position of trees and major shrubs only, in which case 1 : 200 or 1 : 500 might be used. Make sure that the outline of the planting area, at whatever scale, will fit comfortably onto your sheet of tracing paper.

Having drawn the outline shape to scale, place your tracing paper over the graph paper backing sheet on your drawing board. Establishing the scale size of a major grid square will help you to relate to the spread of proposed plants and how much space they will occupy on the ground. At this stage, the exact location of your plan on your tracing paper is not important, because your final drawing for the client will be on a further trace overlay, giving much more information. Label each plant and indicate how many of each species will be planted.

Height and spread

Not all tall plants need to be consigned to the back of the border. Height should be treated like rhythm and should flow backwards and forwards through the borders with carefully sited 'spot' plants, such as verbascums or foxgloves, being allowed to interrupt low planting and relieving monotony. Most catalogues and reference books give the expected height and spread of a plant after five years, and although this varies enormously (both in the books and in reality), plants should be given sufficient space to allow their natural form to be appreciated, as opposed to being overcrowded, when they mature. Shorter lived plants, such as rosemary, could be used as semi-permament stop-gaps.

▶ **How to draw up a planting plan. Use your garden layout plan as a base and trace off the proposed planting areas.**

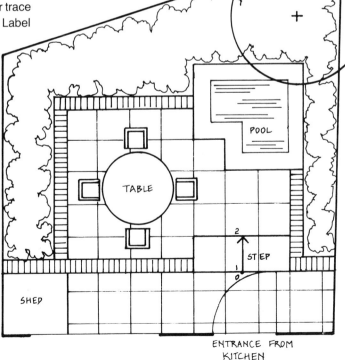

Key planting

Begin by deciding on the location of your key plants – the feature trees and shrubs that you will use to link the planting with the architecture, hard surroundings or landscape – a tree used to soften the angular shape of, for instance, a pond. Either make large freehand circles with a soft, dark pencil or use compasses or a circle template. Try to balance a proposed tree by drawing a group of three shrubs in the opposite corner. At this stage you should not think about what the plants will be, only about balance and counterbalance. Groups of a single type of plant should overlap each other.

Skeleton or structure planting

The next stage is to add the skeleton planting, which will consist of shrubs and climbers to give the garden structure, particularly evergreens, for the winter months. Balance is, again, important. Try to arrange the groups to create movement diagonally from one side of the garden to the other and to help to unify the design. Vary the size of circles to represent a range of different plant species of varying size and to show the space that they will occupy on the soil.

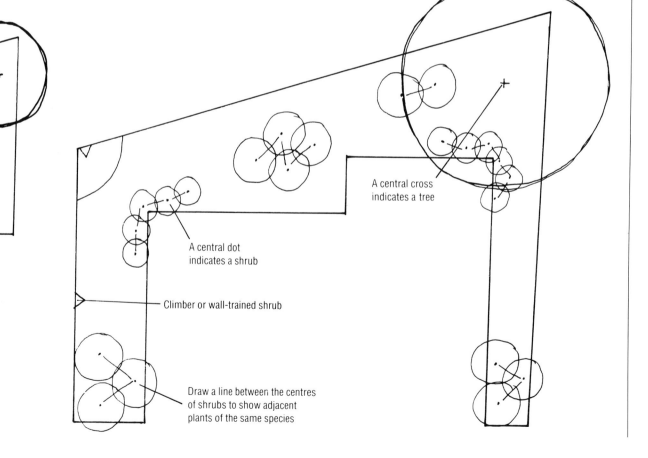

A central cross indicates a tree

A central dot indicates a shrub

Climber or wall-trained shrub

Draw a line between the centres of shrubs to show adjacent plants of the same species

▲ **Add the key plants first – here the tree and the group of three shrubs are placed diagonally opposite. Then work in the evergreen skeleton plants.**

Decorative planting

You can now soften the planting by adding those plants that will play a more decorative role. Try to achieve a ratio of approximately 1 : 3 evergreen to 2 : 3 deciduous plants. It is helpful to shade or hatch the evergreens so that you can see the balance. Choose an evergreen climber for behind a deciduous shrub and vice versa. At this stage you can think not only of shrubs, but also of herbaceous or ground-cover plants, which may remain significant for most of the year.

Study all the shapes you have drawn on the plan and begin to allocate botanical plant names to them, remembering to contrast height, leaf texture and outline shape or form. Try to envisage what your planting will look like throughout the year, bearing in mind that, in addition to evergreens, bark or twig outlines can be very effective when leaves have fallen. Label each plant and indicate how many of each species will be planted.

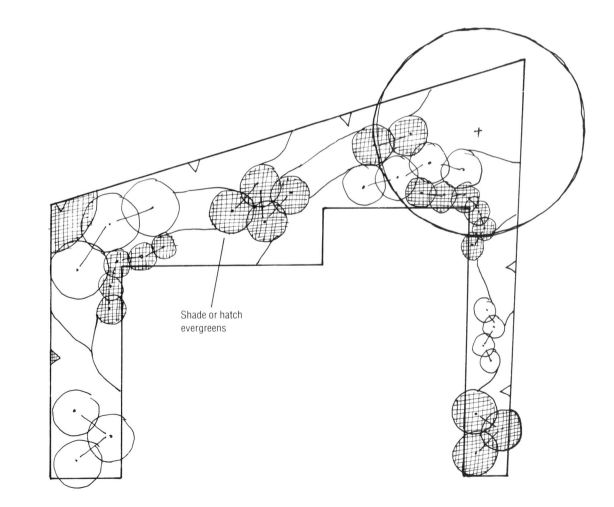

Shade or hatch
evergreens

▶ **Next, add in the decorative plants that will be shown off by the key and structural planting.**

Herbaceous or ground-cover planting

Once all the skeleton and decorative planting is in place, you can concentrate on herbaceous plants, or those smaller scale plants that will filter through the larger specimens. Some herbaceous plants may have strong architectural shapes – acanthus and kniphofia, for instance – or bold leaves, such as hostas. Contrast these strong shapes with softer, fluffier plantings and think about how this herbaceous planting will look against the form, texture and colour of your shrubs and climbers. Try to design the herbaceous areas as drifts rather than as blocks, in which different herbaceous plants weave through the beds and appear to merge into one another.

Label as you go along, stating how many of each, and balancing deciduous with evergreen and, again, repeating groups diagonally. One of the most common faults in planting plans is lack of repetition or the use of too many varieties. This makes a border look restless and unnatural. Either use dots or crosses to indicate the exact planting position or, if space is limited, indicate how many of each with a single line.

Bulbs and infill plants

Bulbs or annuals can be indicated by showing their position and numbers with a broken line, or simply by a line pointer indicating where a group would go. Because bulbs and annuals or infill plants are often used under, or to intermingle with, more permanent plants, it is usually easier to indicate these with a line or arrow rather than labelling them.

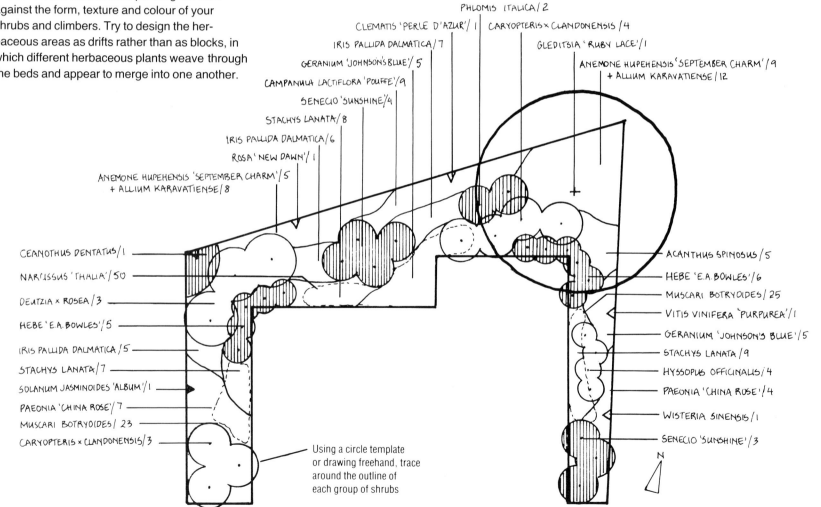

PHLOMIS ITALICA / 2
CLEMATIS 'PERLE D'AZUR' / 1
CARYOPTERIS × CLANDONENSIS / 4
IRIS PALLIDA DALMATICA / 7
GLEDITSIA 'RUBY LACE' / 1
GERANIUM 'JOHNSON'S BLUE' / 5
ANEMONE HUPEHENSIS 'SEPTEMBER CHARM' / 9
CAMPANULA LACTIFLORA 'POUFFE' / 9
+ ALLIUM KARAVATIENSE / 12
SENECIO 'SUNSHINE' / 4
STACHYS LANATA / 8
IRIS PALLIDA DALMATICA / 6
ROSA 'NEW DAWN' / 1
ANEMONE HUPEHENSIS 'SEPTEMBER CHARM' / 5
+ ALLIUM KARAVATIENSE / 8

CEANOTHUS DENTATUS / 1
NARCISSUS 'THALIA' / 50
DEUTZIA × ROSEA / 3
HEBE 'E.A. BOWLES' / 5
IRIS PALLIDA DALMATICA / 5
STACHYS LANATA / 7
SOLANUM JASMINOIDES 'ALBUM' / 1
PAEONIA 'CHINA ROSE' / 7
MUSCARI BOTRYOIDES / 23
CARYOPTERIS × CLANDONENSIS / 3

ACANTHUS SPINOSUS / 5
HEBE 'E.A. BOWLES' / 6
MUSCARI BOTRYOIDES / 25
VITIS VINIFERA 'PURPUREA' / 1
GERANIUM 'JOHNSON'S BLUE' / 5
STACHYS LANATA / 9
HYSSOPUS OFFICINALIS / 4
PAEONIA 'CHINA ROSE' / 4
WISTERIA SINENSIS / 1
SENECIO 'SUNSHINE' / 3

Using a circle template or drawing freehand, trace around the outline of each group of shrubs

N

Plant schedules or lists

Having decided on the plants, take an ordinary jotter or a pad of lined paper and head each sheet according to the listing of the catalogue or the nursery that will be supplying your plants. You may, for example, have one sheet for trees, another for climbers, another for shrubs through to bulbs or annuals. Bamboos, ferns and grasses should be listed separately. You should organize your lists to comply with the catalogue. Put the Latin name of the plant at one side and then the number of plants used in each grouping –

Bergenia purpurascens: 4+15+9 Total 28
Viburnum tinus: 3+5 Total 8

Arrange the lists in alphabetical order, and remember to add the words 'no substitutes', to protect yourself against the supplier running out of stock of a certain plant and sending you something inferior or unsuitable instead.

Labelling

Your planting plan is now ready to be traced or redrawn on a final sheet of tracing paper, and with this comes the laborious business of labelling each planting group. Never use the technique of numbering plant groups and providing a separate key that is so often found in books – by the time you get to 4, you will have forgotten what 1 was.

Annotating your planting plan Always write plant names from left to right. You do not want your client to have to turn the plan upside down to read them.

◀ **Finally, after drawing in herbaceous drifts and areas of bulbs and annuals, label each group of plants. Use Latin names and write in the number of plants in each group.**

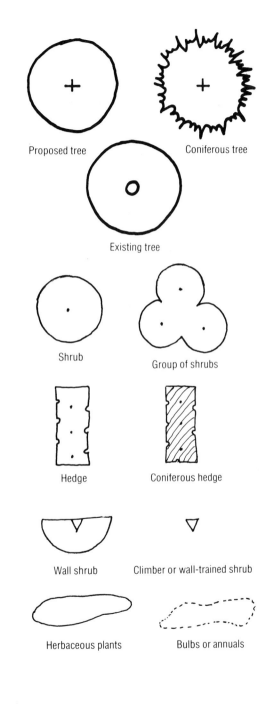

Proposed tree

Coniferous tree

Existing tree

Shrub

Group of shrubs

Hedge

Coniferous hedge

Wall shrub

Climber or wall-trained shrub

Herbaceous plants

Bulbs or annuals

Key to plant symbols

You may help your client to understand the plan if, alongside it, you provide a key to any symbols that you may have used on the plan. It is best to keep these symbols as simple as possible, both to shorten the time that it takes to draw them and to ensure that the plan looks as uncluttered as possible, which will make it easier to read. Freehand drawing and lettering often give a plan more personality than one created with the aid of expensive transfers.

Plant symbols can be used to help distinguish plants of different character. If you decide to use them, aim for simple, stylized outlines and remember that the primary aims of a planting plan are to indicate precisely what plants are to be used and to show exactly where they should be positioned in the area to be planted. Planting plans are supposed to be working drawings, not ones that show every leaf and flower.

In the symbols illustrated, you can see that the centre points of all trees and shrubs are clearly marked. It is important to show this because it indicates the existing stem or proposed planting position. The outline shape of each symbol represents the spread of the plant. In the case of a tree, this is the width of its canopy. It is useful to indicate tree canopies, particularly of existing trees, as their spread will affect what you can plant beneath them. If you are intending to plant under trees, you should also show the plants through the tree canopy. Bold lines used for drawing trees can enhance your plan by helping to give an impression of three dimensions. Normally trees are the most dominant plants in a garden, and they should be drawn with a thick felt tip to indicate this.

◀ **Common symbols used to represent plants on a plan.**

89

Conceptual outline shapes   More realistic shapes with line quality incorporated

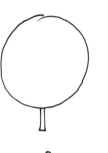
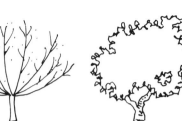

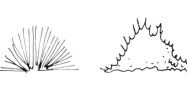

► When working up a planting plan think carefully about the shape and form of plants and try to vary these. You can show how your design achieves this by drawing an elevation of a particular area. Whether you are using simple outline shapes or adding more line quality, try to capture the character of the plants you are using.

Elevation drawings

It is impossible to convey the vertical detail of planting and how it relates to the surrounding architecture or other visual elements on a flat or horizontal plan. Elevations are the easiest way of demonstrating this. They are quick and straight-forward to draw up and can be used to indicate to the client the varying plant shapes and forms. (See also Chapter 9.)

Always indicate on the plan the point from which the elevation has been taken, so that your clients can identify what they are looking at and from where. Choose the location of your cut lines carefully, bearing in mind what you are trying to show. In the example shown here, the planted area chosen for the elevation forms the main view of the garden from the house. When you are drawing up an elevation it can be helpful to work in stages. In the initial stage, the layout and basic forms of trees and shrubs are established. Next the elevation is enhanced by adding herbaceous plants and climbers and developing the shapes.

The elevation need not be to the same scale as the plan drawing, but if it is different, do not forget to indicate this. Elevations usually look best when they are placed above the plan drawing because the plan is normally larger, and there-fore the more dominant of the two. The heavier drawing will look better at the bottom of the sheet.

The elevation can also be used to indicate the long-term changes that will take place in the new garden by overlaying a sheet of tracing paper over the previous drawing to show the anticipated effect of your planting after approximately five years. You can even extend the elevation to show what the planting will look like after 20 years. It may be necessary at that stage to show that some of the original plants may have to be removed. Many of the others will have matured and the space may be overcrowded.

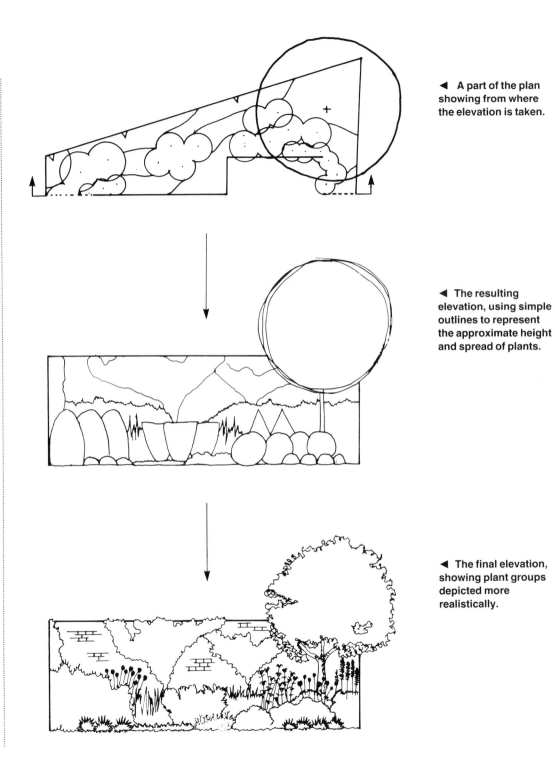

◄ A part of the plan showing from where the elevation is taken.

◄ The resulting elevation, using simple outlines to represent the approximate height and spread of plants.

◄ The final elevation, showing plant groups depicted more realistically.

Planting plans: the final presentation

This should be the culmination of all your work on the planting plan. First, decide on the size of tracing paper that you are going to use. This will normally be A2 (23½ × 16½in) but will vary according to the scale you have used and the dimensions of the planted area. Next, lay your completed rough or previous workings on the graph paper backing sheet and position it carefully, leaving enough space for the elevation drawing to be shown directly above or below, so that it can be related to your plan.

Unless your title block is already positioned on a pre-printed sheet, remember to leave enough space on the right-hand side for this, for the north point and for any notes. You may wish to use the space for notes to describe the thinking behind your proposed planting, or you may simply wish to insert the plant list or schedule. If you are working on several planting plans for the same garden, give each area a different title, such as 'Bed A', 'Bed B' and so on, and label your plant list accordingly. Then, when a large number of plants is delivered on site, the plants can be quickly sorted through and allocated to particular beds.

After tracing and drawing your completed plan, it can be effective to use cast shadows, tone or colour on your drawing. Remember to apply colour only after you have had the work photocopied or printed. Colour may not reproduce from a trace and should always be added to the final printed drawing. If the planted area has been designed to have a particular colour scheme or to look colourful at a certain time of year, this can be indicated by the use of similar colours to enliven the elevation and to help to demonstrate your intention to the client.

However, remember that the plants do not all flower at the same time, and to indicate that they might do would be misleading. The type of finishing treatment you choose will depend on what you have arranged with the client, but it is usually wise to do a little more than he or she actually expects. With experience, you will soon become confident in your ability to communicate your ideas effectively and speedily.

▼ **Techniques for drawing plant shadows.**

Using a circle template as a guide
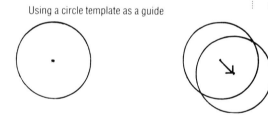

Drawing a pyramidical guideline to reflect a cone-like tree shape

Using a marker pen for quick shadows

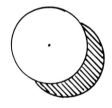

Other ways of enlivening a planting plan

Distinguishing between evergreen and deciduous plants
Show all evergreens with a pencil tone overlaid on the reverse side of the drawing. You should apply the pencil to the reverse side of the sheet so that when it is turned over a hand moving acoss the drawing will not smudge the lead. Always move the lead in the same direction and try not to sharpen or change the lead until the shading work is finished.

Shadows
Shadows can be used to bring depth to a plan by showing relative heights. Check first to see where north lies – the shadows should be in the opposite direction from the sun. The taller the object, the longer the shadow. Shadow effects are discussed in more detail on page 66.

Direction of light determining shadows

▶ **The completed planting plan.**

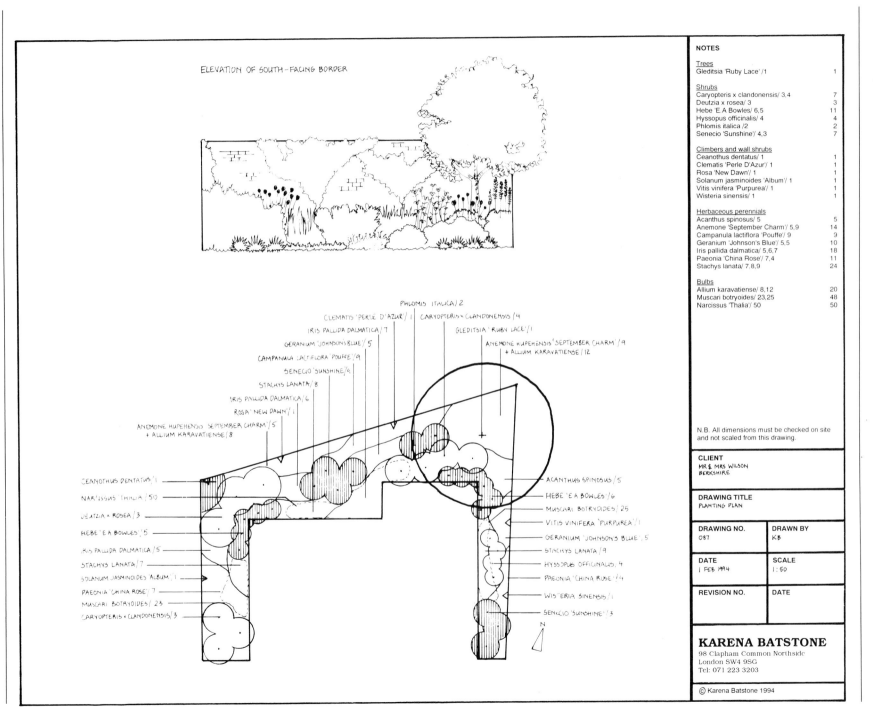

ELEVATION OF SOUTH-FACING BORDER

NOTES

Trees
Gleditsia 'Ruby Lace' /1   1

Shrubs
Caryopteris x clandonensis/ 3,4   7
Deutzia x rosea/ 3   3
Hebe 'E.A Bowles/ 6,5   11
Hyssopus officinalis/ 4   4
Phlomis italica /2   2
Senecio 'Sunshine'/ 4,3   7

Climbers and wall shrubs
Ceanothus dentatus/ 1   1
Clematis 'Perle D'Azur'/ 1   1
Rosa 'New Dawn'/ 1   1
Solanum jasminoides 'Album'/ 1   1
Vitis vinifera 'Purpurea'/ 1   1
Wisteria sinensis/ 1   1

Herbaceous perennials
Acanthus spinosus/ 5   5
Anemone 'September Charm'/ 5,9   14
Campanula lactiflora 'Pouffe'/ 9   9
Geranium 'Johnson's Blue'/ 5,5   10
Iris pallida dalmatica/ 5,6,7   18
Paeonia 'China Rose'/ 7,4   11
Stachys lanata/ 7,8,9   24

Bulbs
Allium karavatiense/ 8,12   20
Muscari botryoides/ 23,25   48
Narcissus 'Thalia'/ 50   50

N.B. All dimensions must be checked on site
and not scaled from this drawing.

CLIENT	
MR & MRS WILSON BERKSHIRE	

DRAWING TITLE	
PLANTING PLAN	

DRAWING NO. 087	DRAWN BY K.B

DATE 1 FEB 1994	SCALE 1:50

REVISION NO.	DATE

KARENA BATSTONE
98 Clapham Common Northside
London SW4 9SG
Tel: 071 223 3203

© Karena Batstone 1994

Labels on plan:

PHLOMIS ITALICA/2
CLEMATIS 'PERLE D'AZUR/ 1
IRIS PALLIDA DALMATICA/7
CARYOPTERIS x CLANDONENSIS /4
GERANIUM 'JOHNSON'S BLUE/ 5
GLEDITSIA 'RUBY LACE'/1
CAMPANULA LACTIFLORA 'POUFFE'/9
ANEMONE HUPEHENSIS 'SEPTEMBER CHARM'/9
+ ALLIUM KARAVATIENSE/12
SENECIO 'SUNSHINE'/4
STACHYS LANATA/8
IRIS PALLIDA DALMATICA/6
ROSA 'NEW DAWN'/1
ANEMONE HUPEHENSIS 'SEPTEMBER CHARM'/5
+ ALLIUM KARAVATIENSE/8
CEANOTHUS DENTATUS/1
ACANTHUS SPINOSUS/5
NARCISSUS THALIA/50
HEBE 'E A BOWLES'/6
DEUTZIA x ROSEA/3
MUSCARI BOTRYOIDES/25
HEBE 'E A BOWLES'/5
VITIS VINIFERA 'PURPUREA'/1
IRIS PALLIDA DALMATICA/5
GERANIUM 'JOHNSON'S BLUE/ 5
STACHYS LANATA/7
STACHYS LANATA /9
SOLANUM JASMINOIDES 'ALBUM'/1
HYSSOPUS OFFICINALIS/ 4
PAEONIA 'CHINA ROSE'/7
PAEONIA 'CHINA ROSE/4
MUSCARI BOTRYOIDES/23
WISTERIA SINENSIS/1
CARYOPTERIS x CLANDONENSIS/3
SENECIO 'SUNSHINE'/3
N

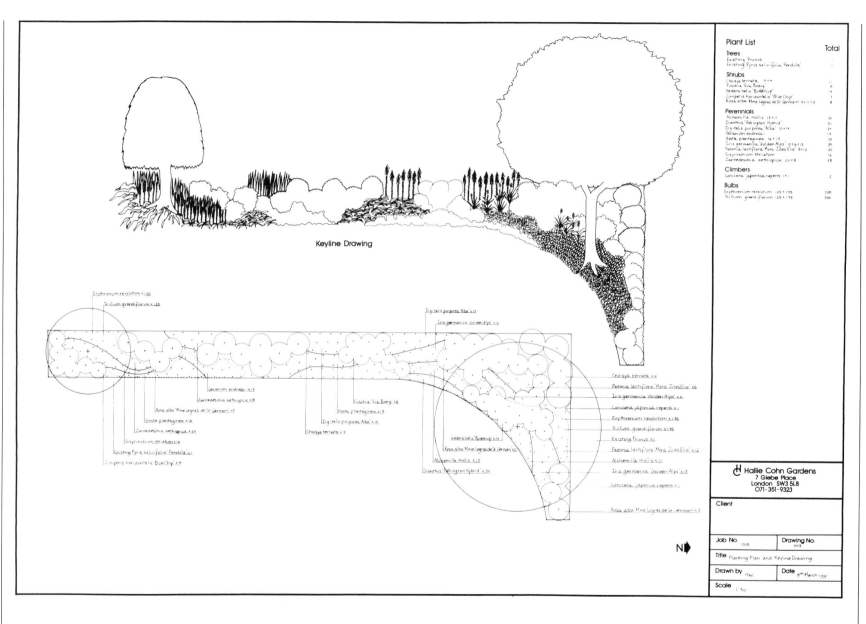

Keyline Drawing

Plant List   Total

Trees
Existing Prunus
Existing Pyrus salicifolia 'Pendula'

Shrubs
Choisya ternata   4+4   11
Fuschia 'Eva Boerg'   6
Hedera helix 'Buttercup'   4
Juniperis horizontalis 'Blue Chip'   3
Rosa alba 'Mme Legras de St Germain' 4+11+3   8

Perennials
Alchemilla mollis 13+11   24
Dianthus 'Oakington Hybrid'   30
Digitalis purpurea 'Alba' 10+14   24
Geranium endressii   17
Hosta plantaginea 16+17   33
Iris germanica 'Golden Alps' 10+6+13   29
Paeonia lactiflora 'Mons Jules Elie' 8+12   20
Sisyrinchium striatum   16
Zantedeschia aethiopica 20+8   28

Climbers
Lonicera japonica repens 1+1   2

Bulbs
Erythronium revolutum 125+175   300
Trillium grandiflorum 125+175   300

Hallie Cohn Gardens
7 Glebe Place
London SW3 5LB
071-351-9323

Client	
Job No. 005	Drawing No. 003
Title Planting Plan and Keyline Drawing	
Drawn by HWL	Date 8th March 1991
Scale 1:50	

▲ In this presentation, the keyline drawing
(elevation) will help the client to visualize the
finished planting. The designer has carefully
selected which groups of plants to emphasize,
contrasting perennials with simplified shrub
outlines. The result is uncluttered and quick
to draw.

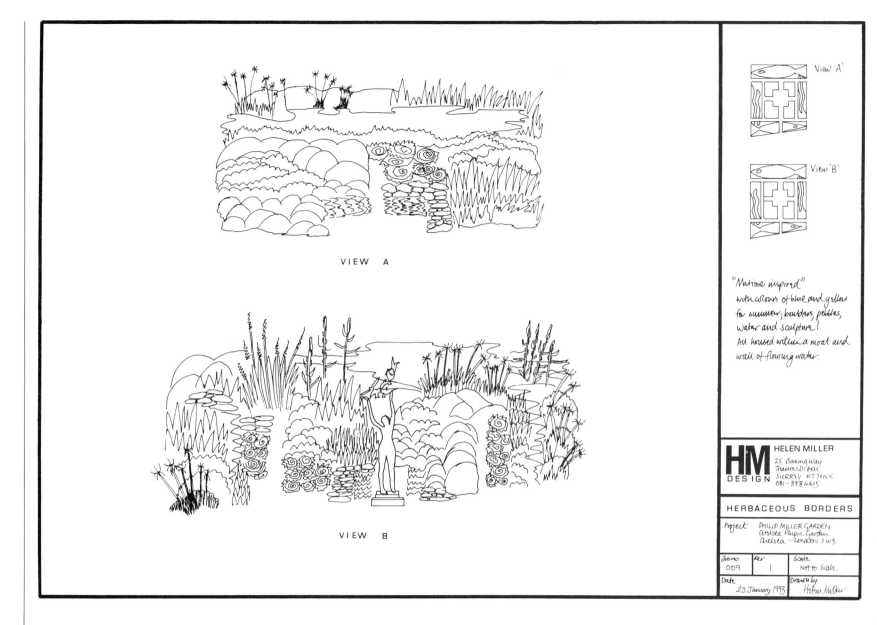

VIEW A

VIEW B

View 'A'

View 'B'

"Matisse inspired"
with colours of blue and yellow
for summer; boulders, pebbles,
water and sculpture!
All housed within a moat and
wall of flowing water.

HM DESIGN   HELEN MILLER
25 Basing Way
Thames Ditton
SURREY KT7 0NX
081-398 4615

HERBACEOUS BORDERS

Project	PHILIP MILLER GARDEN Chelsea Physic Garden Chelsea, London SW3	
Jobno 009	Rev 1	Scale Not to Scale
Date 23 January 1993		Drawn by Helen Miller

▲ These elevations show two views of a 'Matisse' garden, comprised of stone, water, sculpture and herbaceous borders. The designer has achieved a balance of realistic and abstract forms, depicting many of the plants in a stylized way to increase the impact of the design. The simple treatment of the boulders enhances the drawing.

11

Enhancing with visuals

Despite all your work in producing a garden layout and planting plan, from which the garden will be built and planted, your client may have difficulty in understanding your concept. Visuals will help you to explain your intent and, in the case of planting plans, can show the anticipated growth rate at different stages.

For the garden designer, the main purpose of any plan is to communicate ideas to a client. How this is done can vary considerably and the designer usually develops an individual style which can be adapted to the type of work undertaken. The following colour pages show a wide range of work. You should experiment with graphics until you find a method that suits your own ability and which will appeal to your client.

▶ The two plans show the development of a garden design using a grid system to relate the proposed scheme to the existing house structure. (a) The grid chosen for this site derives from the dominant lines – the corners, the edges of the bay window and the conservatory. These lines are subdivided to create a 1-m (1-yd) grid. The design is then developed using the grid lines as a guide, resulting in well-balanced proportions. (b) A rectangular theme based on the grid has evolved for the site. This is appropriate to the style of the house and allows generous proportions for lawn, paved areas and paths. Bringing in the third dimension, a pergola at the far end of the garden provides shade and vertical interest, which is accentuated by the retention of several existing trees.

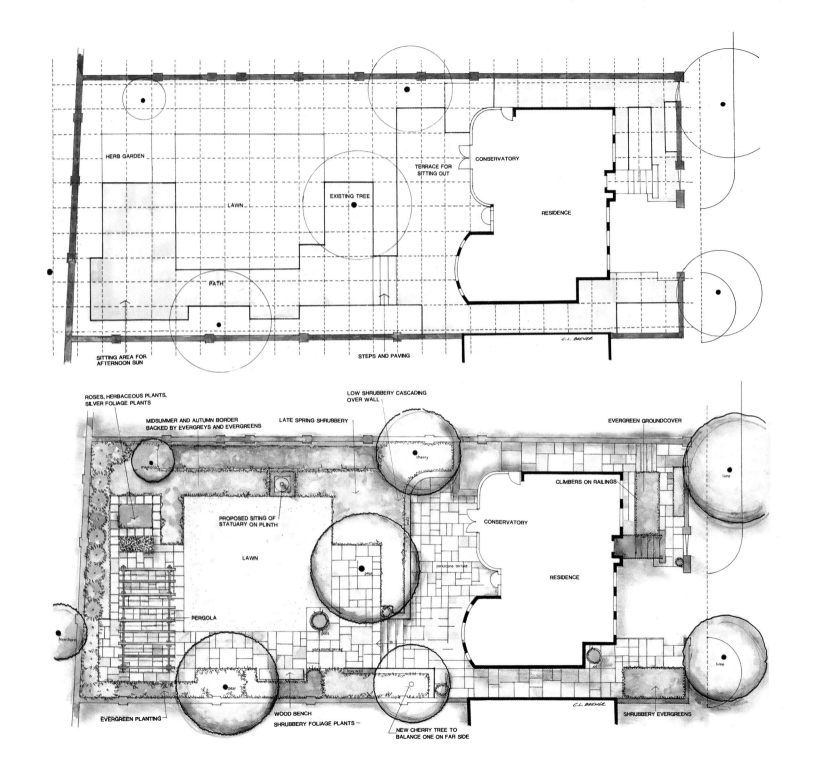

▼ In this static design for a small city garden, timber structures stained peacock blue are softened with plants of silver, blue and purple. The drawing has been watercoloured – a technique that, once mastered, is quick to achieve. The subtle and transparent effect of watercolour, with its implied sense of movement, lends itself very well to most garden plans and drawings.

▶ At the design stage, a planting plan is drawn up to work out the plant grouping and to indicate the location, names and numbers of plants. At the time of planting, each plant will be placed in position according to this plan, which must be legible and easy to follow. Circles are used to define shrubs; a small 'V' shows climbers or wall shrubs. Herbaceous planting is shown as drifts, with a cross or dot indicating in each case how many plants are intended. Note the complete plant list in the information panel.

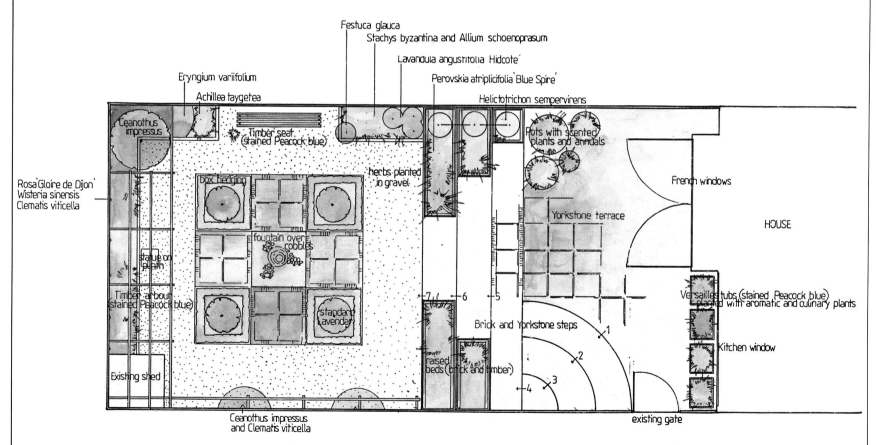

Festuca glauca
Stachys byzantina and Allium schoenoprasum
Lavandula angustifolia 'Hidcote'
Eryngium variifolium
Perovskia atriplicifolia 'Blue Spire'
Achillea taygetea
Helictotrichon sempervirens

Ceanothus impressus
Timber seat (stained Peacock blue)
Pots with scented plants and annuals

Rosa 'Gloire de Dijon'
Wisteria sinensis
Clematis viticella
box hedging
herbs planted in gravel
French windows

Yorkstone terrace
HOUSE

statue on plinth
fountain over cobbles

Timber arbour (stained Peacock blue)
standard Lavender

Versailles tubs (stained Peacock blue) planted with aromatic and culinary plants

Brick and Yorkstone steps
Kitchen window

Existing shed
raised beds (brick and timber)

Ceanothus impressus and Clematis viticella
existing gate

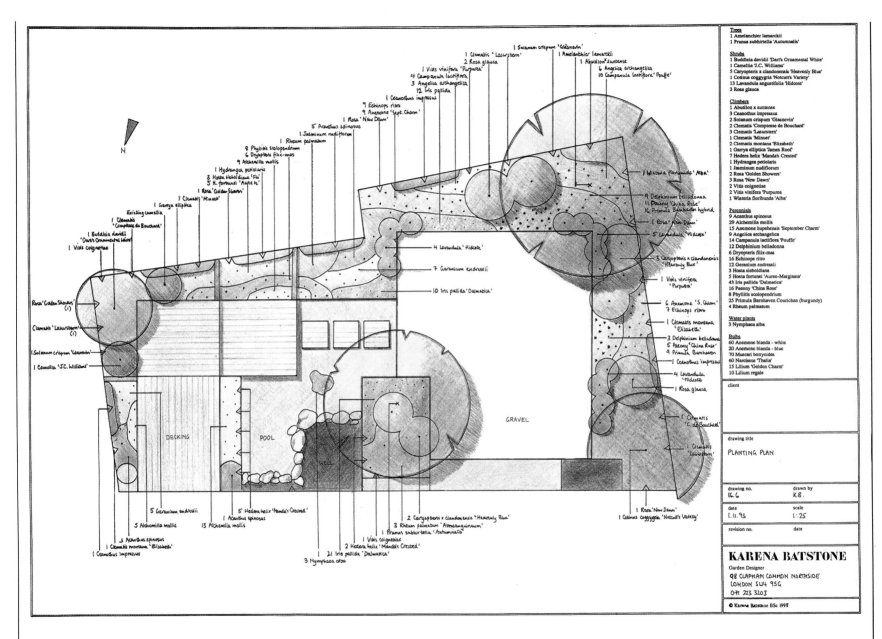

N

Trees
1 Amelanchier lamarckii
1 Prunus subhirtella 'Autumnalis'

Shrubs
1 Buddleia davidii 'Dart's Ornamental White'
1 Camellia 'J.C. Williams'
5 Caryopteris x clandonensis 'Heavenly Blue'
1 Cotinus coggygria 'Notcutt's Variety'
13 Lavandula angustifolia 'Hidcote'
3 Rosa glauca

Climbers
1 Abutilon x suntense
2 Ceanothus impressus
2 Solanum crispum 'Glasnevin'
2 Clematis 'Comptesse de Bouchard'
3 Clematis 'Lasurstern'
1 Clematis 'Minuet'
2 Clematis montana 'Elizabeth'
1 Garrya elliptica 'James Roof'
7 Hedera helix 'Manda's Crested'
1 Hydrangea petiolaris
1 Jasminum nudiflorum
2 Rosa 'Golden Showers'
3 Rosa 'New Dawn'
2 Vitis coignetiae
2 Vitis vinifera 'Purpurea'
1 Wisteria floribunda 'Alba'

Perennials
9 Acanthus spinosus
29 Alchemilla mollis
15 Anemone hupehensis 'September Charm'
9 Angelica archangelica
14 Campanula lactiflora 'Pouffe'
12 Delphinium belladonna
6 Dryopteris filix-mas
16 Echinops ritro
12 Geranium endressii
5 Hosta sieboldiana
5 Hosta fortunei 'Aureo-Marginata'
43 Iris pallida 'Dalmatica'
16 Paeony 'China Rose'
8 Phyllitis scolopendrium
25 Primula Barnhaven Courichan (burgundy)
4 Rheum palmatum

Water plants
3 Nymphaca alba

Bulbs
60 Anemone blanda - white
20 Anemone blanda - blue
70 Muscari botryoides
60 Narcissus 'Thalia'
15 Lilium 'Golden Charm'
10 Lilium regale

client

drawing title

PLANTING PLAN

drawing no.	drawn by
16. 6	K.B.

date	scale
1. 11. 93	1: 25

revision no.   date

KARENA BATSTONE
Garden Designer
98 CLAPHAM COMMON NORTHSIDE
LONDON SW4 9SG
071 223 3203

© Karena Batstone BSc 1993

► Timber decking is the main feature of this plan for a roof terrace. The plan clearly shows the different directions in which the timber should be laid. Two wooden arbours provide shade and privacy, and timber containers are used for the planting. The elevation above the plan shows the different levels and how the features interact.

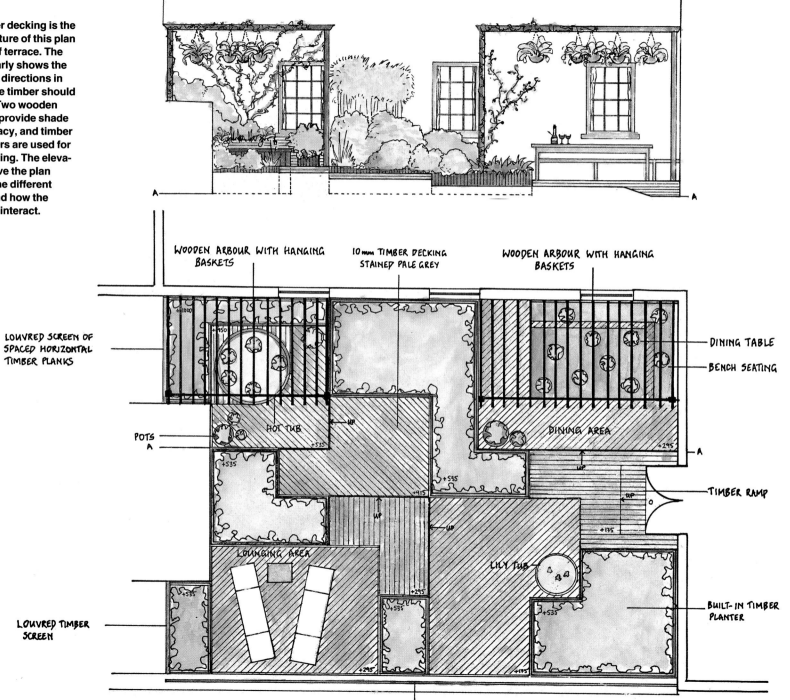

WOODEN ARBOUR WITH HANGING BASKETS

10mm TIMBER DECKING STAINED PALE GREY

WOODEN ARBOUR WITH HANGING BASKETS

LOUVRED SCREEN OF SPACED HORIZONTAL TIMBER PLANKS

DINING TABLE

BENCH SEATING

POTS

HOT TUB

DINING AREA

TIMBER RAMP

LOUNGING AREA

LILY TUB

LOUVRED TIMBER SCREEN

BUILT-IN TIMBER PLANTER

WOODEN RAIL AT 1295mm

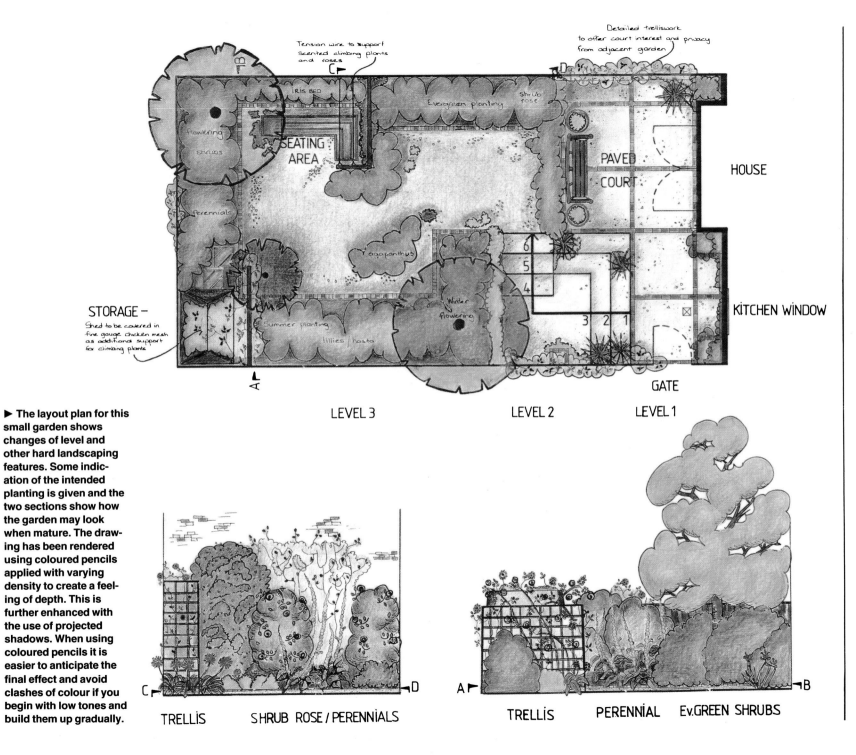

Tension wire to support
scented climbing plants
and roses

Detailed trelliswork
to offer court interest and privacy
from adjacent garden

IRIS BED

Evergreen planting

Shrub
rose

Flowering

shrubs

SEATING
AREA

PAVED

COURT

HOUSE

Perennials

Agapanthus

6
5
4

KITCHEN WINDOW

STORAGE –

Shed to be covered in
fine gauge chicken mesh
as additional support
for climbing plants

Summer planting

lillies / hosta

Winter
flowering

3 2 1

GATE

A

LEVEL 3

LEVEL 2

LEVEL 1

► The layout plan for this small garden shows changes of level and other hard landscaping features. Some indication of the intended planting is given and the two sections show how the garden may look when mature. The drawing has been rendered using coloured pencils applied with varying density to create a feeling of depth. This is further enhanced with the use of projected shadows. When using coloured pencils it is easier to anticipate the final effect and avoid clashes of colour if you begin with low tones and build them up gradually.

C

D

TRELLIS   SHRUB ROSE / PERENNIALS

A

B

TRELLIS   PERENNIAL   Ev.GREEN SHRUBS

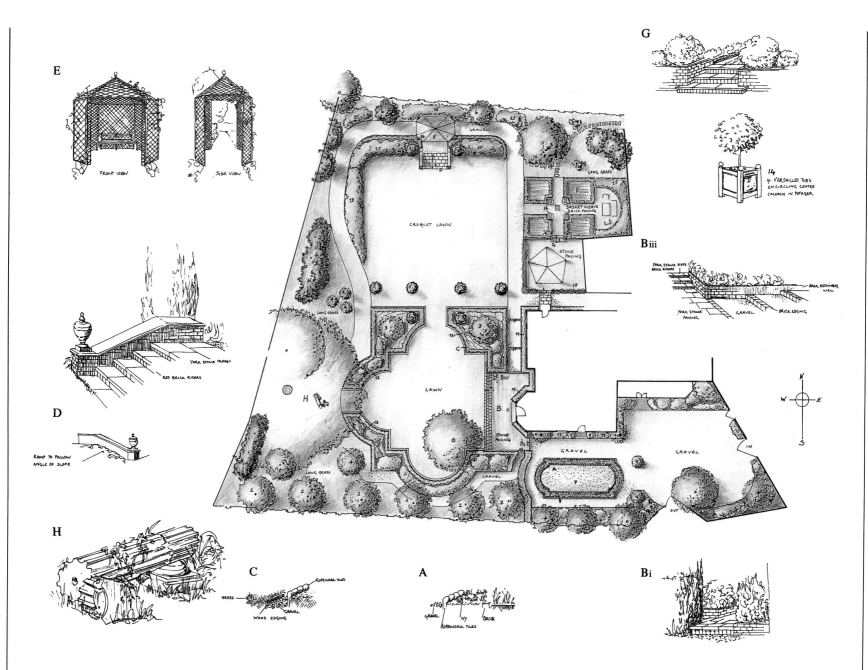

E
FRONT VIEW   SIDE VIEW

G

14
4 VERSAILLES TUBS
ENCIRCLING CENTRE
COLUMN IN POTAGER

B iii
YORK STONE STEPS
BRICK RISERS
BRICK RETAINING
WALL
YORK STONE
PAVING   GRAVEL   BRICK EDGING

YORK STONE TREADS
RED BRICK RISERS

D
RAMP TO FOLLOW
ANGLE OF SLOPE

H

C
GRASS   ROPEWORK TILES
GRAVEL
WOOD EDGING

A
GRAVEL   IVY   BRICK
ROPEWORK TILES

Bi

N
W   E
S

(Plan labels:) GRAVEL · LONG GRASS · BASKET WEAVE BRICK PAVING · STONE PAVING · CROQUET LAWN · LONG GRASS · LAWN · STONE PAVING · GRAVEL · LONG GRASS · GRAVEL · GRAVEL · IN · OUT

▲ The client may find a garden layout plan difficult
to understand. These enticing illustrations for the
formal garden clarify the proposals and each
sketch is numbered to show the precise location.

If you find freehand sketching difficult, these little
diagrams can easily be adapted from a book or
catalogue, and they may help sell the concept.

► This anoxometric drawing illustrates the circular theme used to give a sense of movement in a rectangular garden. This type of drawing shows how retaining walls and steps create changes of level. It can also be used to check on proposed heights and widths. Loose outline shapes indicate the contrasting form and texture of the planting, while pencil shading has been applied to give a three-dimensional effect. The inclusion of a garden seat gives a sense of scale.

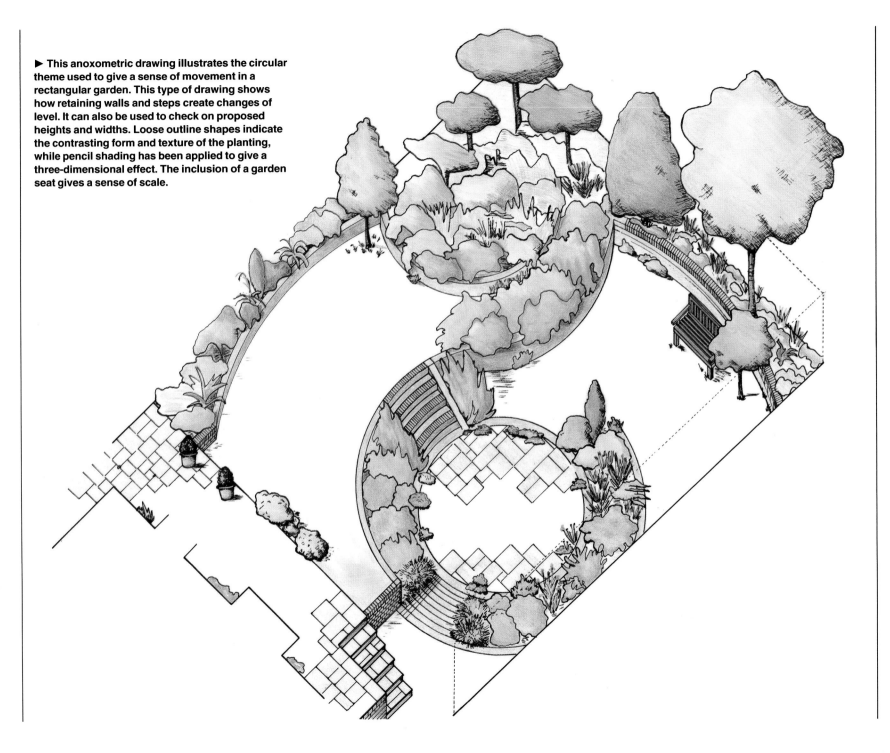

a

b

This page has a planting plan and two photographs, taken a year after planting, that illustrate how a design concept for a garden is realized. Photograph (a) is an overall view of the garden and (b) is the south-west corner.

▲ The planting in this garden has been designed so that the flowering herbaceous plants are set off against a framework of shrubs, incorporating existing ones such as the box square in the foreground. Although the colour scheme is predominantly red, an infill of blue gives interest until the planting matures.

▲ The surrounding ragstone walls and overhanging foliage plants provide a background for this border. At their flowering peak in early summer bulbs are used to vary the colour scheme.

▶ This finished drawing is simply a coloured-up version of a working drawing, in which all the shrubs are drawn as circles and the herbaceous plants as fluid shapes interwoven between them. Using coloured pencils to add tonal contrast and a sense of light, the well-balanced composition is effectively brought to life.

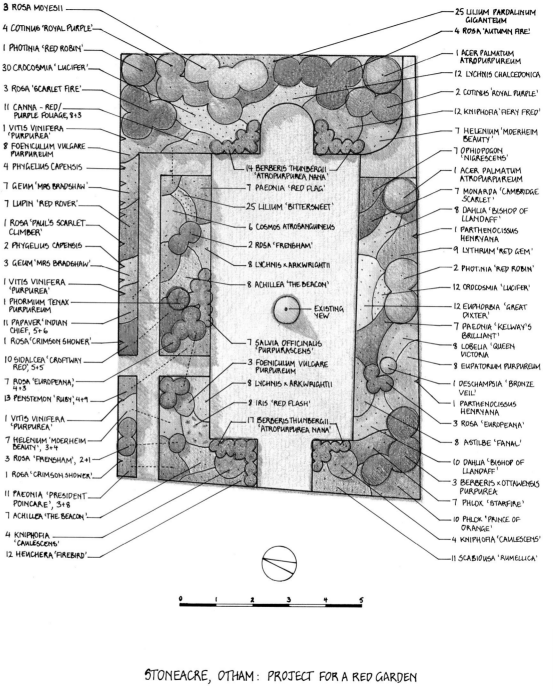

STONEACRE, OTHAM: PROJECT FOR A RED GARDEN

DESIGNER : ANTHONY DU GARD PASLEY

Orthographic projections

This is a method in which you draw objects by producing a series of flat views of their sides, showing all their features drawn to scale. This is done by projecting them up from your plan. An elevation is one type of orthographic projection. Other kinds are axonometric and isometric projections.

Axonometric projections

An axonometric drawing is a three-dimensional, measured drawing that, by being projected up from a scale plan, will give height and depth to your design. It will provide a view of the garden as seen from above and at an angle – similar, as it were, to viewing it from a neighbour's second-floor window. It will help you to see how the components of the garden – buildings, walls, steps and fences – relate to each other. If you have forgotten to think through, for instance, the height of a retaining wall or the height of risers and widths of the treads of a flight of steps this will become obvious when you are trying to project them. Once you understand the underlying principle, an axonometric drawing is a quick and easy method of checking your design or any details, such as the construction of a pergola or pool. The most difficult task in this type of drawing is to depict plants in a lifelike manner.

The drawing is created by tilting your plan 45° from the horizontal, projecting up all the vertical elements at the same scale as the horizontal elements on the plan and then connecting the tops of the verticals. Note that all the horizontals will be drawn as diagonals, but all the verticals will remain vertical.

Drawing an axonometric projection

1. Using your parallel rule or T-square and a 45° set-square, fix down your garden layout plan at an angle of 45° with, if possible, the lowest level of the garden or the terrace nearest the bottom of the page.

2. Stick a sheet of tracing paper over this.

3. Use your scale to measure the vertical lines around the boundaries or the exterior of the site and project up from each corner the height of any structure – building, walls, fence and so on – at these points.

4. Use your set-square to join up these points, showing the structure that is nearest to you in a broken line. This will indicate its presence, but allow you to 'see' through it on the drawing. Your garden plan will now have become three-dimensional.

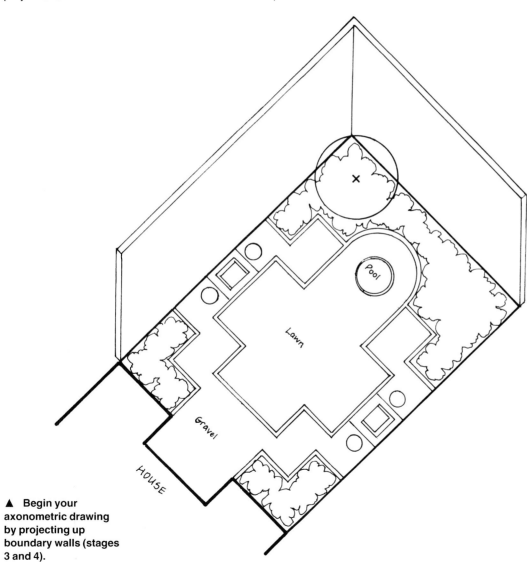

▲ **Begin your axonometric drawing by projecting up boundary walls (stages 3 and 4).**

5. Proceed in the same way with the interior of your plan, starting at the lowest level or terrace, which should, if possible, be nearest to you and, working up gradually through each construction and change of level. Some more distant features may be hidden behind those in the foreground. At present show only hard landscaping; the plants can be added later. In this drawing each vertical measurement should be taken from the level of your starting point, but if your garden includes several changes of level, it may be easier and quicker, once the first level has been drawn, to slip the tracing paper overlay up or down to adjust to the height of the new level. This will save having to remember to add on, or subtract from the earlier dimensions each time.

All circles on your plan, such as round pools, pots or tables, will appear as true circles in an axonometric projection, although they will need to be set up to find the centre point of what will become a raised circle.

6. When you have finished drawing all the hard landscaping, including pots, pergolas and garden furniture, there may be so many lines that your drawing looks rather confused. It is sometimes easier to lay a further sheet of tracing paper over the drawing and trace only the lines that you actually want.

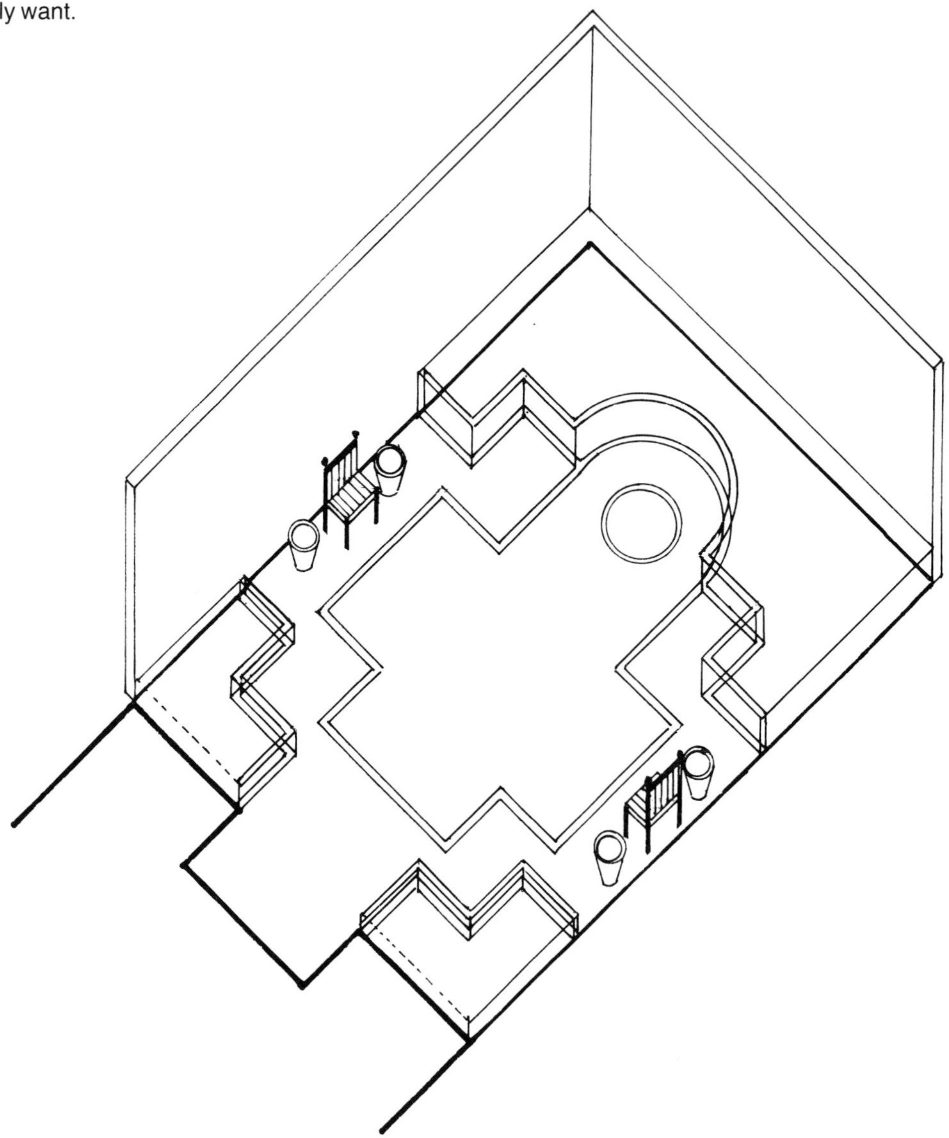

▶ **Projecting up
internal structures
(stage 5).**

106

7. The planting can be added to the same sheet or done on an overlay, the two being combined for the final drawing. Begin by moving to the lowest part or terrace of the garden and locate the planting position of an adjacent tree (or shrub). Project a vertical line up from the centre point of the trunk to the height of the top of the tree, marking on the trunk the point at which the tree canopy begins. Using that point as the centre, draw a circle to indicate the width or spread of the tree canopy. Normally the tree canopy will narrow at top of the tree, so you should draw another circle, using the tallest point of the tree height as the centre of the circle. Join up the two. This will leave only a small amount, or none, of the tree trunk showing, and although it may look a little odd, it is correct. Proceed in the same way for the other trees and shrubs.

8. Climbers and herbaceous plants are normally indicated by showing an outline of their height and spread. Avoid confusing the drawing with too much detail of stems, leaves and so on.

▶ **Plants added on an overlay (stage 7).**

107

Axonometric gridded paper of different scales is
available from good artists' shops and can
be very helpful in setting up an axonometric
projection.

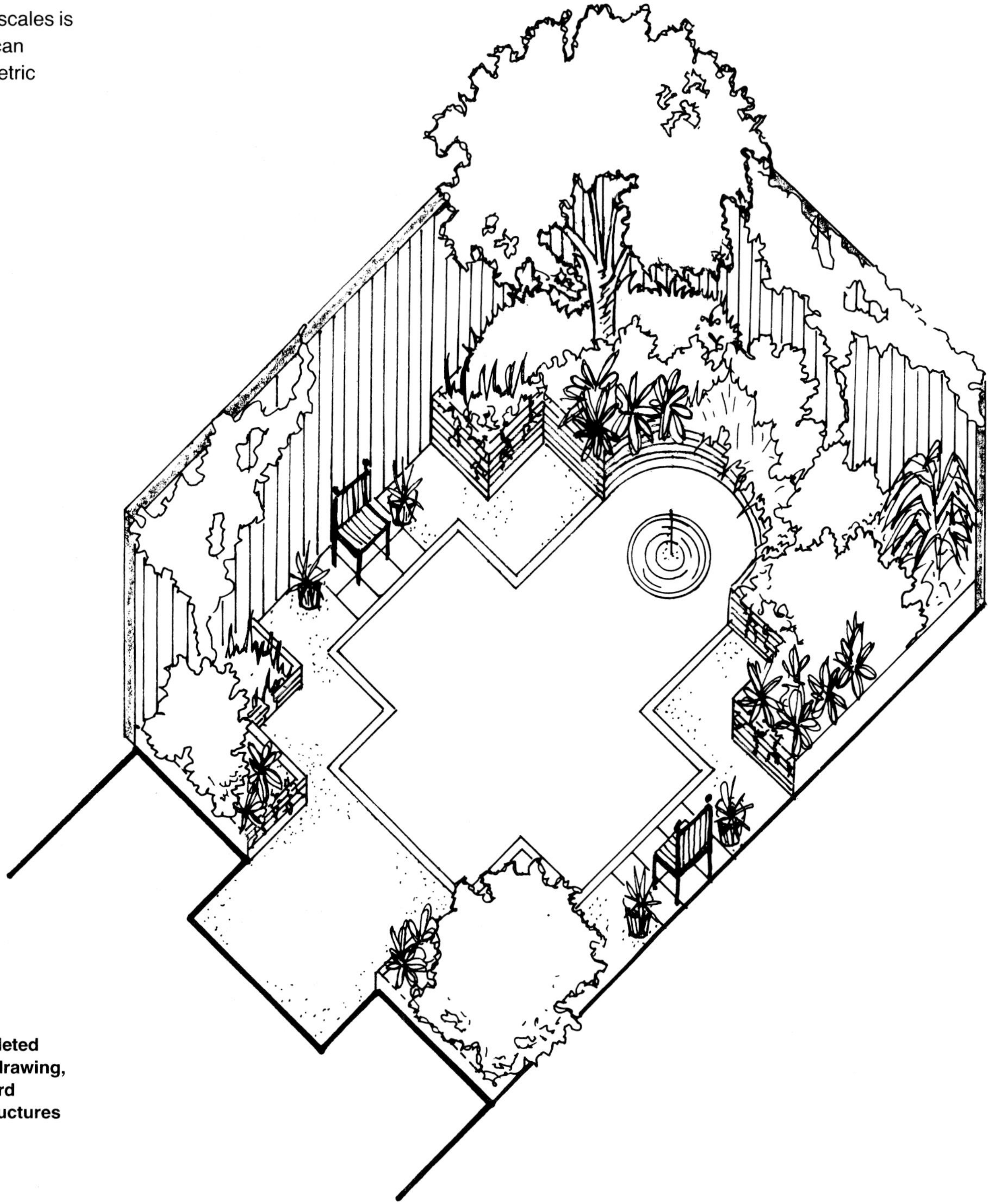

▶ The completed
axonometric drawing,
combining hard
landscape structures
and planting.

Examples of completed axonometric drawings.

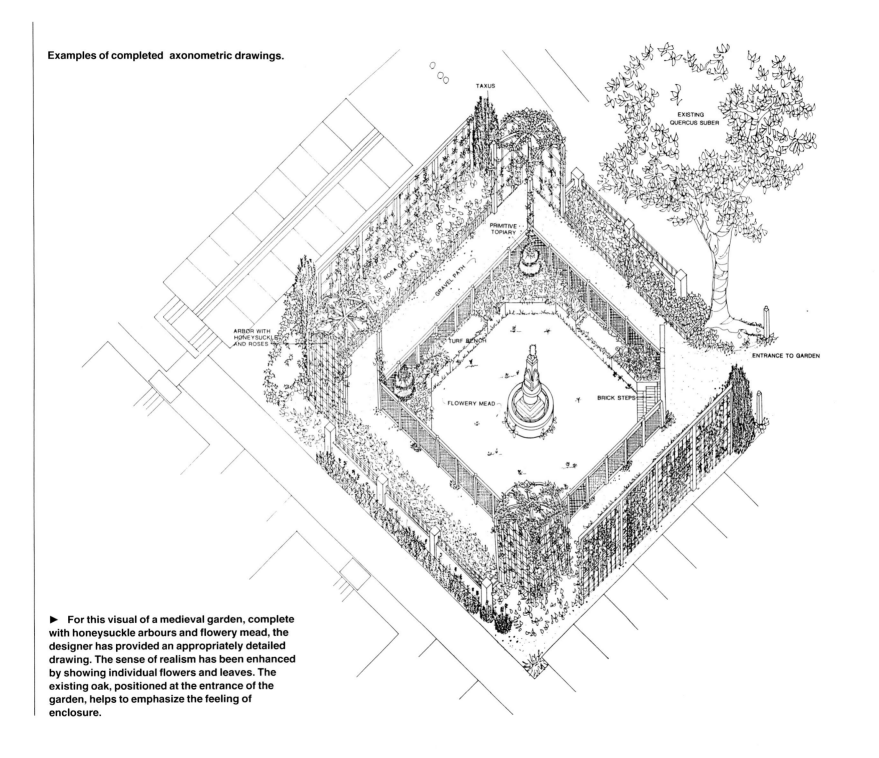

TAXUS

EXISTING QUERCUS SUBER

PRIMITIVE TOPIARY

ROSA GALLICA

GRAVEL PATH

ARBOR WITH HONEYSUCKLE AND ROSES

TURF BENCH

ENTRANCE TO GARDEN

FLOWERY MEAD

BRICK STEPS

▶ For this visual of a medieval garden, complete with honeysuckle arbours and flowery mead, the designer has provided an appropriately detailed drawing. The sense of realism has been enhanced by showing individual flowers and leaves. The existing oak, positioned at the entrance of the garden, helps to emphasize the feeling of enclosure.

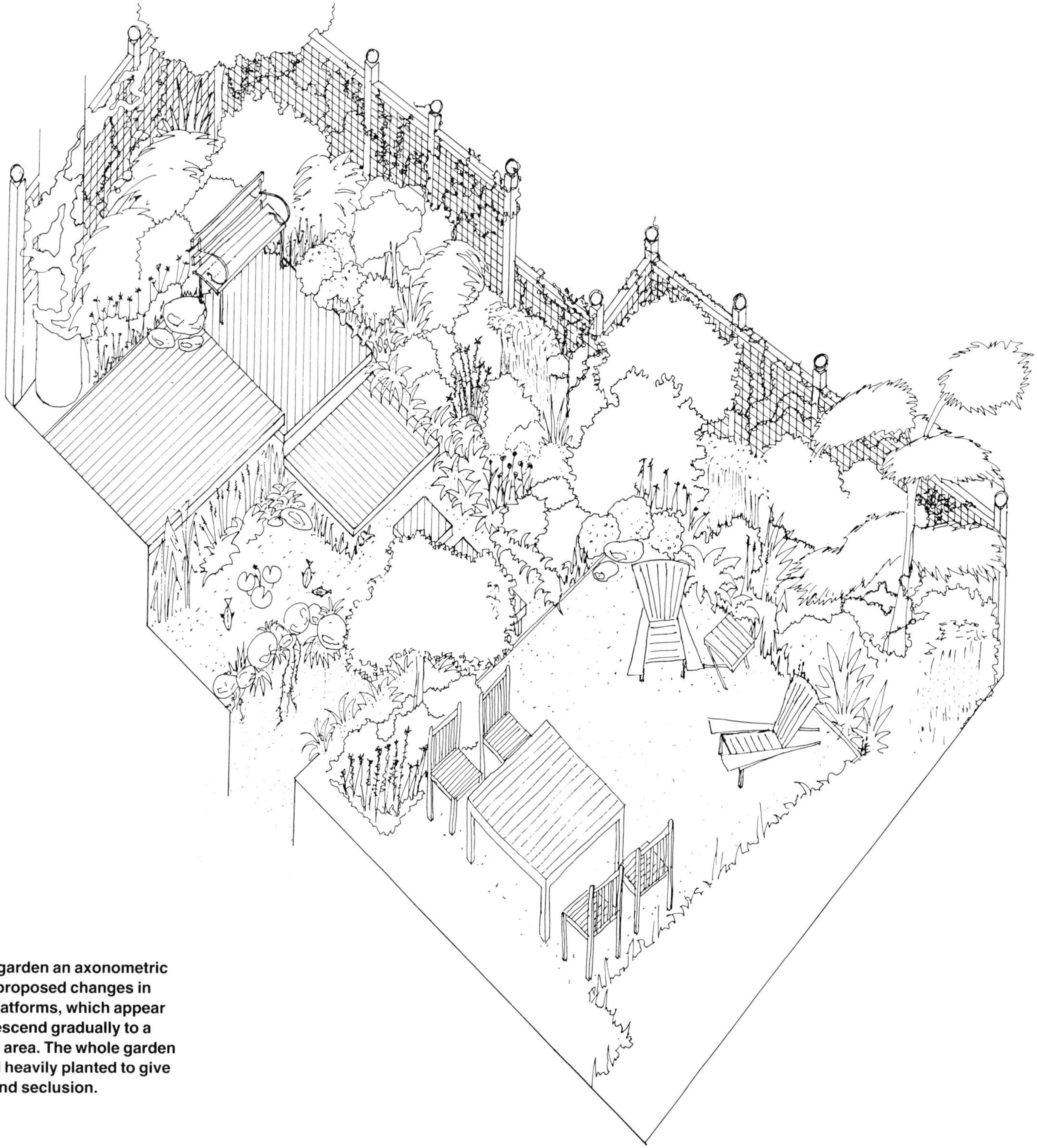

▶ In this design for a city garden an axonometric
drawing clearly shows the proposed changes in
level. A series of decking platforms, which appear
to float over a deep pool, descend gradually to a
gravelled dining and sitting area. The whole garden
is surrounded by trellis and heavily planted to give
an atmosphere of privacy and seclusion.

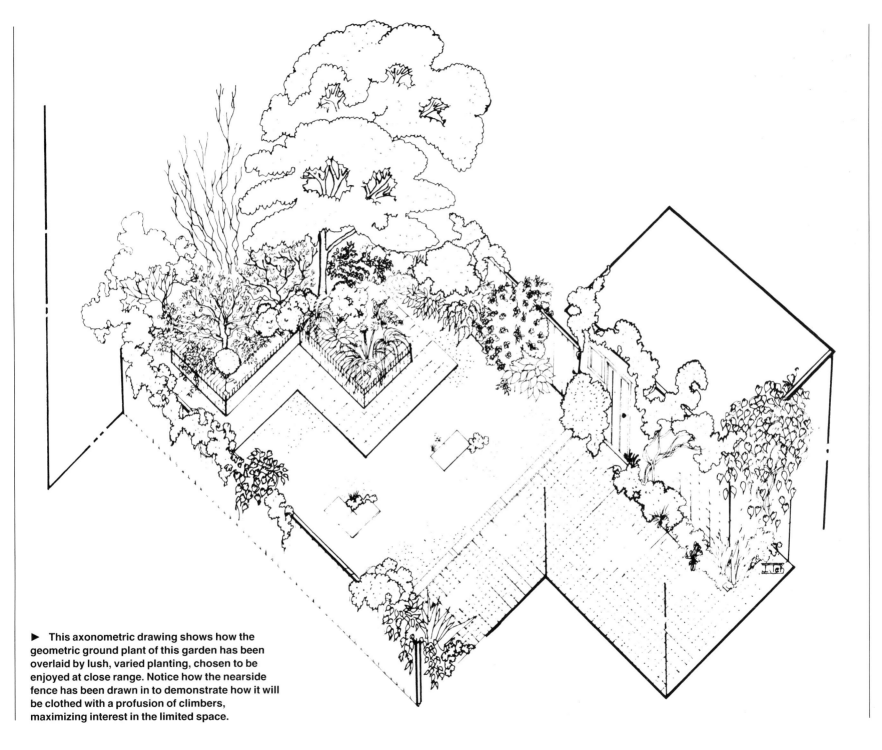

▶ This axonometric drawing shows how the geometric ground plant of this garden has been overlaid by lush, varied planting, chosen to be enjoyed at close range. Notice how the nearside fence has been drawn in to demonstrate how it will be clothed with a profusion of climbers, maximizing interest in the limited space.

Isometric projections

This is similar to axonometric but instead of a 45°
set-square, you will need to use a set-square
with angles of 30° and 60°. If a plan includes
shapes at 45°, an isometric plan will show more
than an axonometric one. In fact, the projection
can be taken at any pair of angles that add up to
90°, even 75° and 15° as long as the angles are
adhered to once they have been chosen.

In projections other than axonometric projections,
circles will appear as ellipses, and to achieve this
you may need to set up a rectangular framework
of straight lines or use an ellipse template.

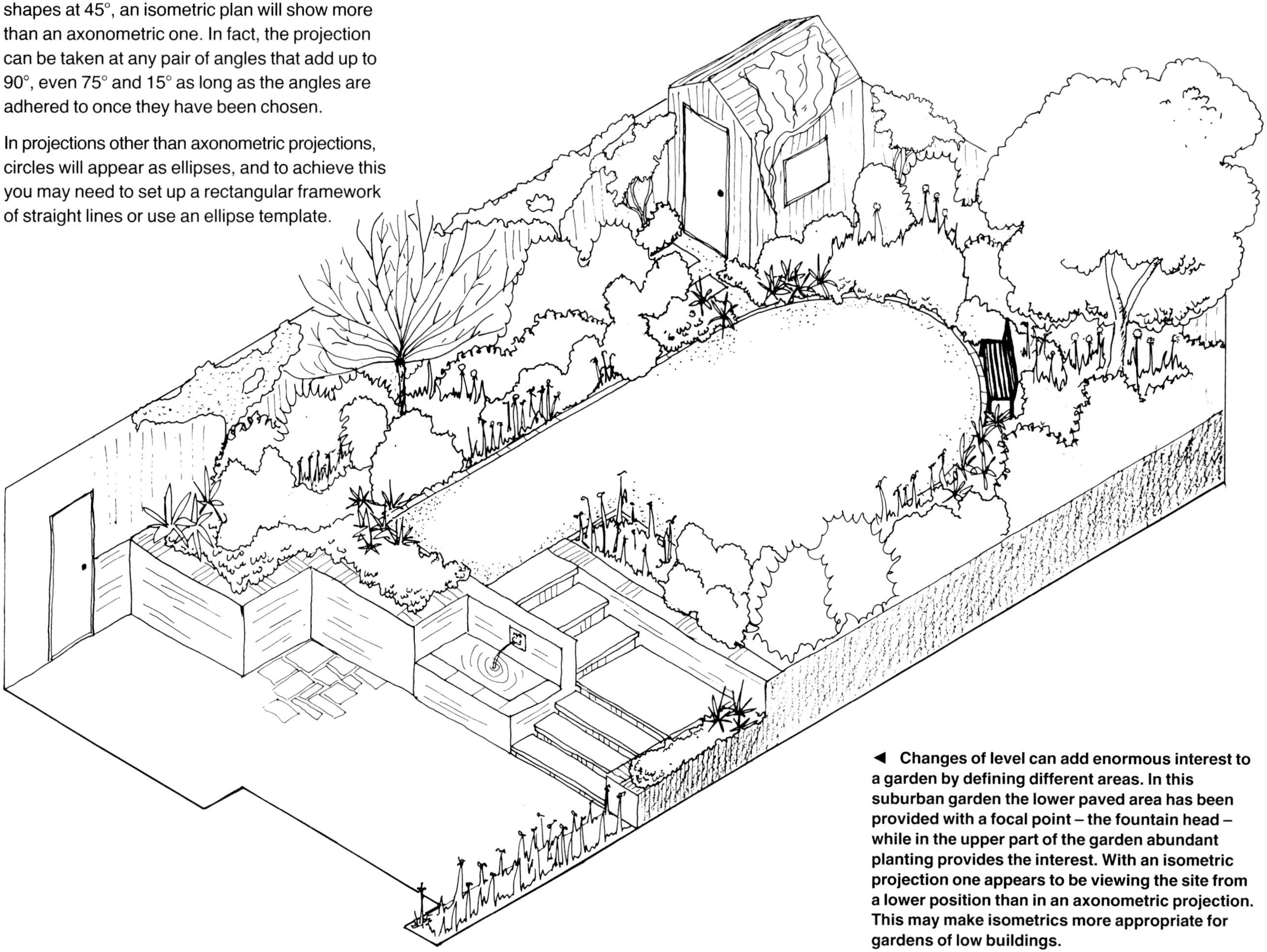

◄ **Changes of level can add enormous interest to
a garden by defining different areas. In this
suburban garden the lower paved area has been
provided with a focal point – the fountain head –
while in the upper part of the garden abundant
planting provides the interest. With an isometric
projection one appears to be viewing the site from
a lower position than in an axonometric projection.
This may make isometrics more appropriate for
gardens of low buildings.**

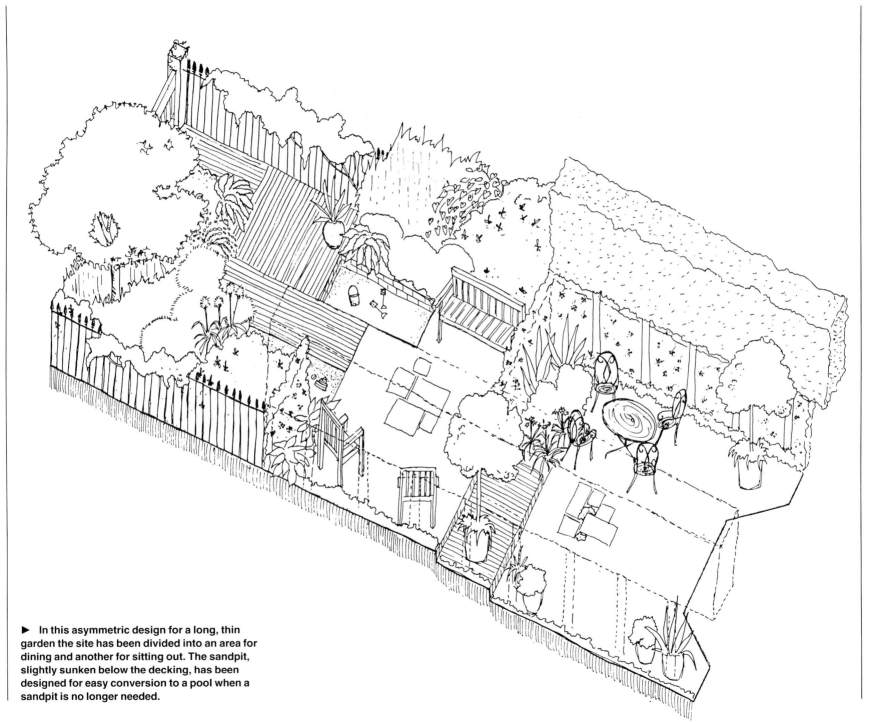

► In this asymmetric design for a long, thin garden the site has been divided into an area for dining and another for sitting out. The sandpit, slightly sunken below the decking, has been designed for easy conversion to a pool when a sandpit is no longer needed.

113

Perspective drawings

A perspective drawing is also three-dimensional but unlike a projection it gives a realistic view of the garden as seen from a chosen point and reproduces what is seen in real life. Any part or parts of the garden can be chosen for a perspective drawing, and two sketches usually accompany an average plan. It does not matter if your first attempts at perspective are fairly rough. With practice they should soon communicate your design concept.

A one-point perspective is the simplest to draw. It means that the garden, or part of it, is viewed head-on from a fixed point, called the standpoint. From this fixed point, all parallel lines converge into an imaginery point on the horizon, called the vanishing point, which is located on a plane known as the picture plane.

Preparing a perspective drawing

1. Fix a sheet of tracing paper over your plan. Using your garden layout plan, choose the area that you wish to depict by choosing your standpoint and your picture plane.

2. Draw a central line, the sightline, from the standpoint to your picture plane, which will be in the centre of your cone of vision, or the splay of view that is being depicted in the drawing. This must be no more than 60° wide.

3. Draw an elevation of the view and establish an eyeline on the picture plane. This will be a horizontal line at a level at which your eye might rest naturally. This may be 1 metre (yard) or more from the ground. If you are viewing the garden from a balcony or upstairs window, it might be 4 metres (yards) high. The point at which the eyeline and the sightline intersect is the vanishing point.

4. Now draw a line from the vanishing point through each corner of the picture plane.

▶ **After selecting a standpoint and picture plane on the plan (stage 2), draw an elevation of the chosen view and establish an eyeline on the picture plane (stage 3).**

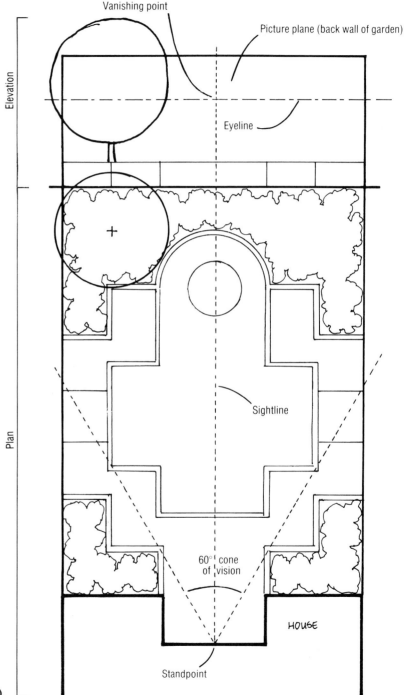

5. Divide up the horizontal and vertical sides of the picture plane at fixed intervals – perhaps every 1 metre (yard) – and draw lines from the vanishing point through the fixed points.

6. Go back to your plan and measure the distance on the plan between the standpoint and the picture plane.

7. Mark this on the eyeline to either side of your vanishing point.

8. From that mark, draw a line through to the nearest lower corner at the picture plane, and continue drawing it across your 1 metre (yard) radiating lines.

9. At the point where your diagonal crosses each radiating line in the ground plane of the projection area, draw in a horizontal line to establish one more grid on the ground plane.

10. Construct a vertical 1 metre (yard) grid by drawing a vertical line perpendicular to each horizontal grid line at the edge of the ground plan.

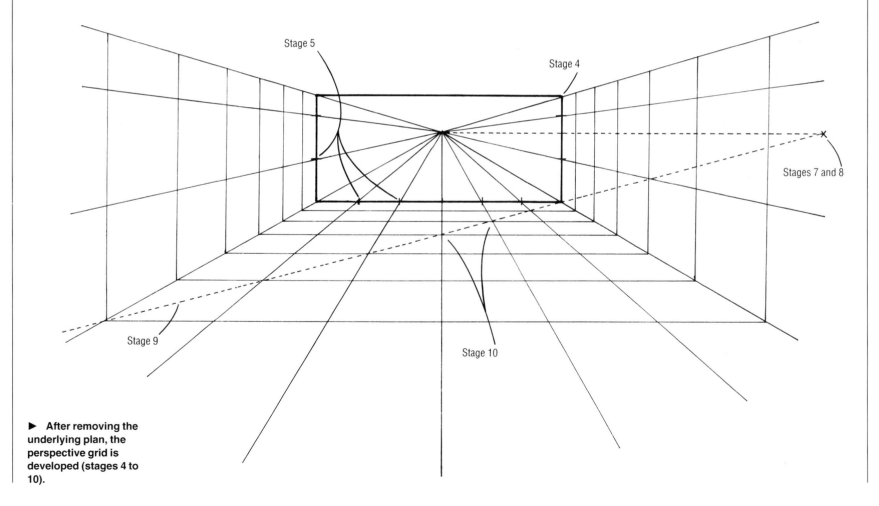

Stage 5

Stage 4

Stages 7 and 8

Stage 9

Stage 10

▶ **After removing the underlying plan, the perspective grid is developed (stages 4 to 10).**

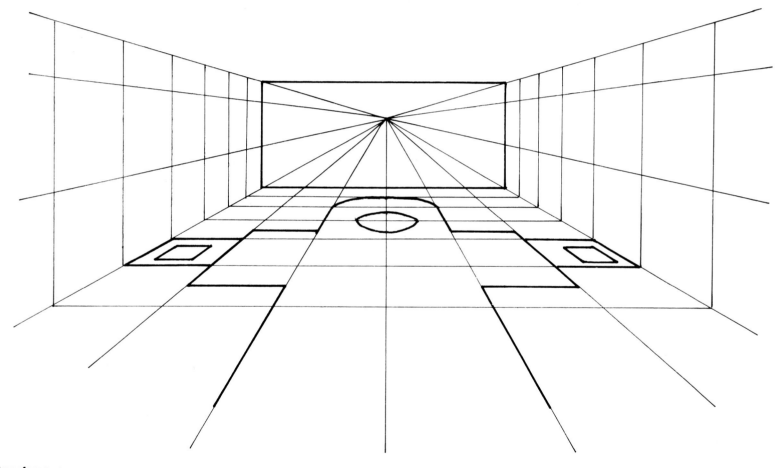

► Transfer your garden layout plan onto the ground plane grid (stage 11).

11. Transfer your garden layout plan to this grid.

12. You are now ready to project the elevation drawing forwards using your vertical grid to determine the correct heights of each element.

13. Link up all the sides of the objects by following a line from each elevated point to the vanishing point.

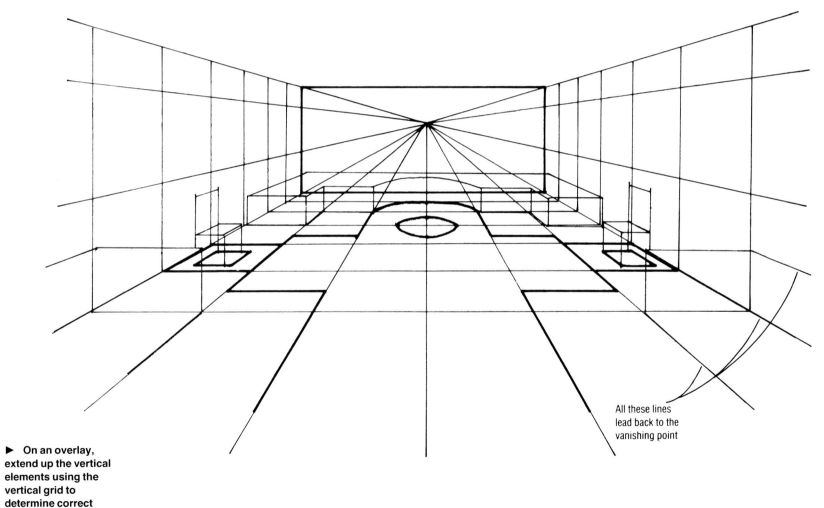

All these lines lead back to the vanishing point

▶ **On an overlay, extend up the vertical elements using the vertical grid to determine correct heights (stage 12).**

14. To work up a final drawing, lay over a further sheet of tracing paper and trace over the drawing, eliminating the grid lines to show all objects, including trees and shrubs.

To help bring your perspective to life you can use shadows and reflections, varying the thickness of your pens or pencils. Treating the plant material in different ways can give the impression of form and texture, and the inclusion of people will help your client to identify with scale. It is worth mastering perspective so that you can present your client with an enticing drawing.

Two-point perspective is used to draw objects that are at an angle rather than head-on to the viewer. It is a more complex method of construction and is rarely needed by the garden designer.

▲ **The finished perspective with plants added. Note how the realism of the drawing has been increased by giving more detail and textural interest to the plants in the foreground than to those further back.**

Examples of completed perspective drawings.

▲ This perspective drawing was achieved by sketching over an enlarged photograph of the existing site. When there are elements in the site that will remain unchanged – such as the house and mature trees – this method is an effective way of explaining proposals.

▲ This detailed drawing has been drawn up to demonstrate the profusion of plants intended for the site. When creating visuals of this kind it is better to concentrate on the impression given by the drawing as a whole, rather than attempting to represent every plant accurately.

► **This perspective drawing illustrates part of a plan shown on page 80. Using a one point perspective, a symmetrical design of this kind can be drawn quickly, showing horizontal and vertical elements that are not obvious on a plan.**

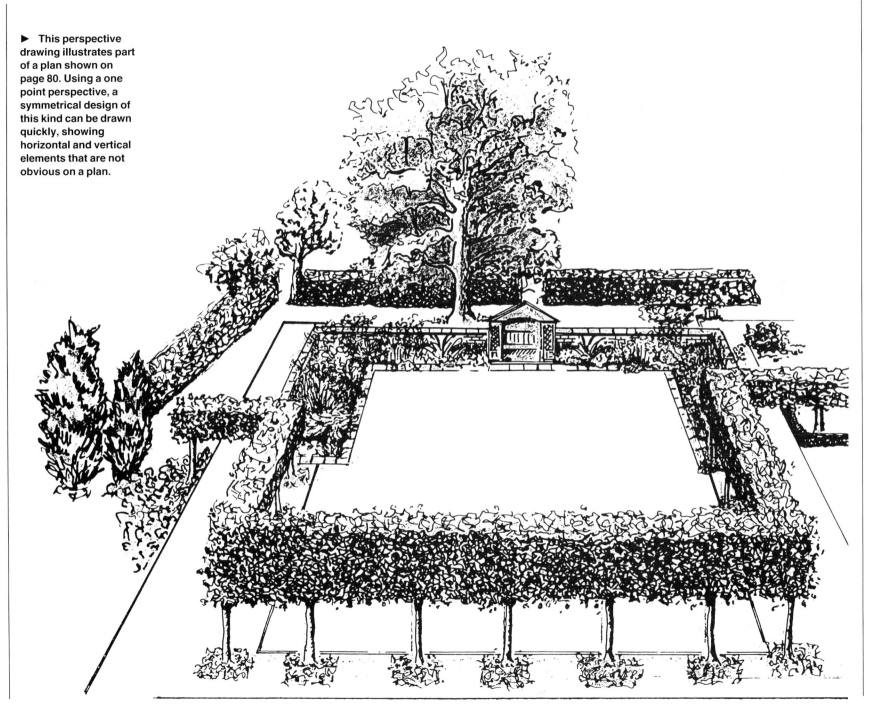

▲ The inclusion of the house in a visual often helps to give a sense of scale and may be useful in showing how the design will relate to existing features.

Sketching over photographs

This is probably the simplest method, but it does not produce quite the same professional finish. However, it is a quick and easy way of presenting 'before' and 'after' effects, and it can also be used to illustrate a report. If you intend to use this technique, it would be sensible to take suitable photographs when you make the survey, and it usually means taking carefully composed shots of the garden as viewed from the house, and a view looking back towards the house from the opposite end of the garden. The site itself and your immediate assessment of it will probably suggest other shots that you might use.

When the film has been developed, prints can be used as they are or they can be enlarged. The prints can also be enlarged and reproduced on paper with a photocopier, which is cheaper but not so effective.

Preparing the sketch

1. Fix your photographs or photocopy to your backing sheet.

2. Lay over it a sheet of tracing paper.

3. Refer to your plan and trace over all objects shown in the photograph that you wish to retain. By referring back to your survey it should be possible to have some idea of the scale at which you are drawing.

4. Using another sheet, refer to your garden layout plan and draw your proposals. You may be able to draw them almost to scale. If, for instance, you know the height of an existing garden shed, a proposed pergola could be shown at the same height. Continue until you are satisfied that everything you propose is shown.

▶ **Sketches over photographs are useful for communicating ideas to your clients. They are both quick to draw and easy to understand.**

Quick perspectives

One very simple method of creating a perspective drawing without having to draw perspective lines or use perspective charts can be achieved by using a camera. Both one- and two-point perspectives can be created in this way.

First, place your outline garden plan flat on a desk or table. Then, standing above the plan and at an angle to it, focus your camera so that the plan fills the frame. Take several photographs at different angles. When the photographs have been developed, you can enlarge them on a photocopier to the size that you want your finished perspective drawing to be.

Choose one of the photos and trace over the plan lines. Now extend up the vertical lines in proportion to the width of the plan objects to complete the drawing.

◄ Photograph of a plan drawing in perspective.

▲ For this method of creating perspectives, position your camera at an angle to the plan to set up the perspective view.

► The completed visual with verticals extended in proportion to object widths.

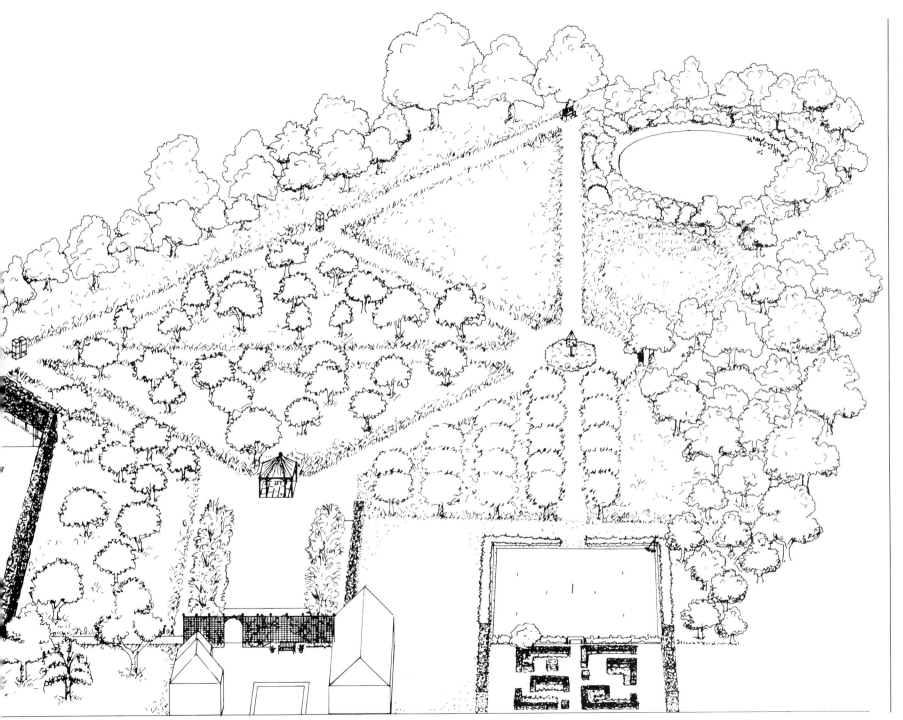

12

Reproducing and presenting work

Most drawings are originated on tracing paper. Alterations may easily be made on it, but it is fragile and there is only one original, so the finished drawing must be copied to give to the client. It will thus become a negative to be photocopied or printed. This reproduction of the original drawing can then be rendered – that is, it may be coloured or treated in such a way as to explain the concept more clearly.

An established designer often has a particular presentation technique, and it is worth spending some time thinking this through, and deciding what overall effect you wish to achieve. There are many ways of presenting work, and the method you choose will be determined by the intended recipient and the available budget.

Methods of drawing and the various media were discussed in Chapter 1 but it may be useful to recap as follows.

Lines may be drawn in pencil, ink or a combination of both, provided that any pencil work is carried out in a fairly hard lead, which will give a crisp line when reproduced. Choose a type of lead that will not smear and, if possible, cover the pencil lines with a clean sheet of tracing paper to avoid smudging if your hand has to move across them.

Technical pen ink, which is normally used with drawing pens, gives a crisp, professional effect, but this comes only with continued practice. There are several recommended sequences which help to give a good finish. This is the most commonly used one:

▼ After working out the nib sizes to be used for different elements, start inking in using your finest nib size. Draw all the horizontal lines first, then the verticals and then all other lines. Repeat this exercise with the thicker nibs until you have completed the drawing.

1. Work out nib sizes for all drawn items before commencing the drawing – for example, 0.7 for boundaries, 0.5 for trees.

2. Starting with the horizontal lines, draw them in with the finest pen nib size to be used on the drawing.

3. Draw in all vertical lines with the same fine nib.

4. Draw in all other lines.

5. Draw in all the horizontal lines in the next nib size.

6. Repeat this exercise with all vertical and other lines.

7. Increase the nib sizes until all work, right up until the thickest nib size, has been executed.

8. Work over the final drawing as little as possible by covering the paper or sections not currently being worked on with clean tracing paper.

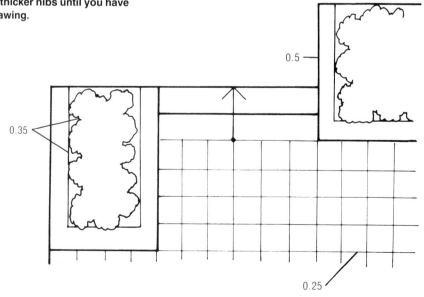

0.5

0.35

0.25

Common faults when using technical pen ink

- very fine ink lines may not reproduce when printed
- tense or shaky hands give an uneven effect
- if the surface of the tracing paper has to be worked over, either by scratching out with a scalpel or by using an eraser, future lines drawn in ink may tend to bleed unless the surface has been restored; the best way of doing this is to burnish the paper with your thumb nail
- if ink is used directly over pencil lead, the lead may prevent the ink from being absorbed evenly by the paper, resulting in an uneven or smudgy line; trace the final drawing over a completed drawing or series of smaller drawings
- because inferior quality tracing paper will not stand up to being worked on, use a medium or stout thickness for final drawings
- do not use coloured pens or pencils on tracing paper because colour may not reproduce when printed or it may cause the tracing paper to stretch or buckle, which will show when reproduced.

Reproducing the drawings

All final tracing paper drawings, whether of the garden layout plan or of sections or details, will need to be reproduced for the client and the contractors. Sometimes several copies of each are required, to be given to the different contractors or professionals involved. These final drawings will have taken many hours of work and would be costly to redraw. Therefore, each final tracing paper drawing should be classed as an original, and treated with respect. Store them flat in a plan chest away from excessive heat, damp or sunlight, and take them out of your office in a closed portfolio or rolled in a drawing tube, having made sure that each one has your name, address and telephone number written clearly on the outside so that it can be returned if it is lost or mislaid. Do not send or take them to the reprographic office or printers unprotected and rolled up with only an elastic band or piece of masking tape holding them together. Rain may damage them or even the perspiration from your hand will be absorbed by the tracing paper, and will then be reproduced for the client.

There are three main ways in which your original drawings can be reproduced, but you should understand the differences so that the reproduction will serve its purpose. The methods are copy negatives or prints (dyelines or photocopies).

Copy negative
This is a reproduction of the drawing as a negative, and is usually produced on:
- **tracing paper**, when it is hard to tell which version is the original
- **lacquered tracing paper** on which the original is printed on the reverse of the drawing and which is easily torn or damaged
- **sepia film**, in which the drawing is also printed on the reverse side, but which is stronger and less easily damaged.

Copy negatives can be useful if, when the hard landscaping drawing has been completed, you want this to remain as an original but want to do the planting plan on an exact copy. If the plan is copied, the original can remain as the hard landscaping drawing, perhaps to be copied again before any revisions or alterations are made on the original, or for use as a basis for the 'setting out' drawing from which the contractor will measure out the garden on site. Never revise or alter the original. If you do, you will no longer have a record of what you have done, and your client may well decide, despite having requested a revision or alteration, that it is best to return to the original design.

Before beginning to scratch out or erase any unwanted material on copies of the originals, check whether the work has been printed on the front or reverse side by testing a small area. If you attempt to scratch anything out without making this test, it is all too easy to end up with a large hole. If the original has been copied on blue intense film, the original may be easily distinguished because it will have been printed on the reverse side in brown, while new work carried out in ink will show up as black. When they are copied, however, the two different colours of ink will reproduce the same.

Prints
There are two main ways in which copies of the original can be printed on to paper – dyelines and photocopies.

Dyelines
In modern reprographic offices, the dyeline print has been largely superseded by the photocopy, but in some ways dyeline prints are preferable – they are cheaper and the finished effect is less harsh. The dyeline process needs a transparent negative – i.e., the drawing on tracing paper – to

be passed through rollers in contact with diazo paper, which is sensitive to ultraviolet light. The roller is a tubular lamp, which emits this ultra-violet light. Good ink originals or negatives come up as almost black lines on white paper, while fainter pencil drawings may show some background tint. This can be a grey or bluish tone and the technique used to be called a blueprint. The roller machine may need to be adjusted to give a lighter or darker contrast, and often a good printer will test a strip to begin with, then adjust the machine before printing the complete sheet.

However, if your final drawing consists of pieces of paper which have been stuck down with tape, these will show up on the dyeline, although not on photocopies.

Using colour on dyeline prints If the drawing is to be used for presentation work or to give to your client, it should be as crisp as possible, and colour or tone may need to be applied afterwards. When colour is to be added, the original should be printed on heavier paper, because felt-tip pens or watercolours can make lightweight paper buckle. Reprographic offices do not always hold stocks of this thicker paper, and it must either be ordered in advance or brought in with the original drawing and given to the printer. If watercolours are to be used, it may be best to execute the original in pencil so that the ink lines do not overrule the pastel shades. It is also wise to have the original reproduced on watercolour paper to gain the best effect.

Originals can be printed on a wide range of papers – cartridge, ozalux, which gives a wipeable effect with dull sheen, but on which colour can be difficult to apply, or art grain, which gives an antique or bumpy effect, the ink reproducing in dark brown as opposed to black, which can be appropriate for historic sites. Coloured card can also be used, but this must be thin enough to pass through the rollers.

Photocopies

Many of the larger offices now have photo-copying machines, although few will take the largest paper sizes. Photocopying is a photographic process and produces a crisp drawing. Again, the copy can be made on different types of paper, provided these will pass through the machine, although the ink often does not hold on heavily textured paper.

Reductions or enlargement The original drawing may also be reduced or enlarged. You may need to do this because the original drawing is to be reproduced as part of a matching set, perhaps to fit into a portfolio in which the other original drawings have been carried out on a different sized sheet or at a different scale.

A drawing can often look crisper and more professional when it is reduced, although it is important that the content remains clear and the handwriting legible.

Many photocopying machines have a facility for reducing or enlarging, but before you commit a drawing to be altered in size, make sure that any writing will still be legible. Reductions sometimes improve the overall appearance of a drawing, but if the handwriting is shaky, enlargements will emphaize this. Do a test run to make sure that the process will suit the work and the writing.

▼ **Folding techniques for standard paper sizes to ensure that the title block remains visible after folding.**

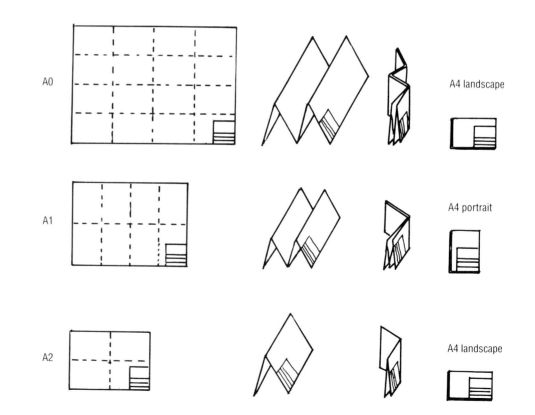

A0

A1

A2

A4 landscape

A4 portrait

A4 landscape

Reducing or enlarging will also alter the scale of the drawing, so any notes on scale size will need to be erased or removed before the copy is made, and the adjusted scale – perhaps 1 : 50 reduced to 1 : 100 – written in afresh.

Microfilm

Some large practices record drawings on micro-film, which is a photographic process by which miniature transparencies are made of the drawings. This method of storage takes up little space but is expensive and unlikely to be used by many private designers.

Finishing processes

Once copies of the drawing have been reproduced as dyelines or photocopies, they may be toned, coloured, mounted and sealed, or encapsulated – your choice will depend on how the work is to be presented to the client.

After the copies have been printed, they should be folded and taken or sent as required, but if the plan and the visuals have been printed on thicker than normal paper, you may not wish to fold them. With normal dyeline or photocopied plans or drawings, the paper should be folded so that the lower right-hand corner contains an inform-ative title block. The folding of plans can indicate to a fellow professional the training and experi-ence or lack of it. Knowing how to fold, or unfold, a plan is important when you are struggling to open it on a windy, exposed site, or when you are folding a large batch of drawings to send to the various people involved.

It is always better to talk a client through a plan rather than to send it through the post, leaving the client to make his or her own interpretation. Many clients are unwilling to admit that they cannot read a flat plan, and even though it may be accompanied by visuals, there are always points that you should clarify personally.

Presenting your work

The most commonly used methods of presenting your work are:

- **a folded dyeline print or photocopy of your original** (this is the most usual way of presenting work)
- **an extra-stout print**, which is more expensive but may later be framed by the client and should not, therefore, be folded
- **a portfolio**, containing a variety of presentations, including plans, photographs and so on, which is normally used to obtain future work.
- **a print mounted on stiff card or hardboard and heat-sealed around the perimeters** for exhibition or display purposes
- **a print, possibly reduced or enlarged, encapsulated in clear, firm plastic**, which is a lighter but very durable way of displaying and storing exhibition drawings

Dyeline prints

When they are exposed to light dyeline prints fade quickly and can soon become yellow and unreadable. To prevent this they should be stored flat in a clean, dry and dark place. A plan chest is ideal, but a cupboard or drawer will suffice. Work can also be stored in a flat portfolio, which can be slipped under a desk or bed.

Photocopies

Photocopies do not fade so easily, but they should be stored in a similar way.

Extra-stout prints

Extra-stout prints that have been rendered or coloured can be very effective, and they may be used to present the client with more sophistic-ated work. The garden design may sometimes be commissioned as a retirement or anniversary gift, and a drawing printed on this thicker paper gives the recipient the option of having the work framed or mounted as a record of the occasion.

Portfolios

Compiling a portfolio can be an effective way of displaying completed designs that can be shown to future clients to illustrate the type of work they may expect from a designer. Clients can look through the portfolio, perhaps pointing out a design that appeals to them. As each job is completed, the relevant drawings can be slipped into a portfolio, each in its own plastic sleeve, as a record of the work. Before they are included in a portfolio, drawings or prints can be enlarged, or, more usually, reduced. Photographs of the site before work begins and after completion can also be mounted on card, perhaps with descriptive captions, to show future clients what can be achieved. The 'before' and 'after' photo-graphs can also be used as a record of the quality of work carried out by the contractors. Costs of the various elements – paving, walls, planting and so on – could also be included so that a future client can judge the level of costs involved. If you do this, include the date of execution, as these costs will not remain static.

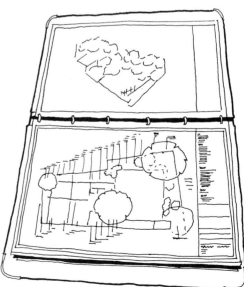

▲ **A typical A2 portfolio.**

Exhibiting work

If work is to be exhibited, perhaps at an international flower show or art exhibition, it may be necessary to have it mounted and framed, or heat-sealed, which can be particularly important if the exhibition is to be held outdoors, when a damp atmosphere can have a catastrophic effect on paper. Even if the display is under canvas, damp can still ruin drawings. An alternative method is to have the work encapsulated or sealed within two sheets of clear plastic. The drawings remain light to transport and to store, and the sealed work can be mounted on a wall with adhesive stickers. The overall effect of the work will often depend on the background against which it is exhibited, so this should be taken into account when a display is planned. It is best to find out from the exhibition organizers exactly what space is available and what it consists of – whether it is nothing more than a bare stretch of grass on which you will need to erect your own display, or a background of portable lightweight screens. The display can be drawn to scale in diagrammatic form so that the sequence can be seen.

If work is to be submitted for hanging, then this diagrammatic plan should accompany it, including clear instructions and leaving no margin for error by those organizing the display. A separate board, with the name of the designer or the title of the work, may be mounted above the drawings and occasionally a small box for printed cards for interested viewers may be included. Much future business can be generated by exhibiting at appropriate events, and the display should be as professional and distinctive as possible.

Number each piece of artwork on the reverse side

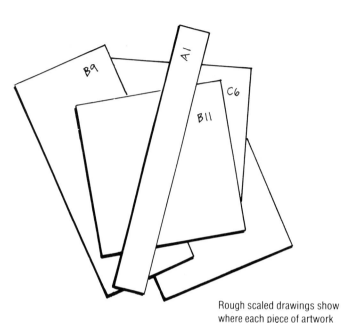

Rough scaled drawings show where each piece of artwork will be located on the display boards

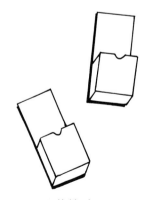

Holder for name cards

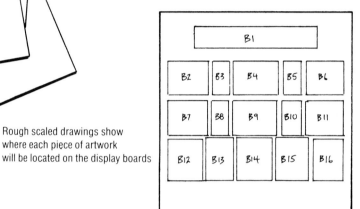

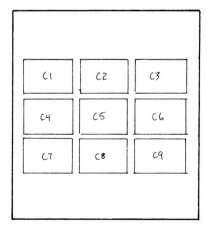

▶ Planning the layout for an exhibition.

▶ The final display.

13
Establishing your own practice

The size and way in which a garden design practice operates can range from a small, part-time consultancy to an international practice that designs and builds gardens. Some designers begin by replanning their own garden, then go on to work for admiring friends and acquaintances until they have built up their own clients. Others have trained through landscape architecture or garden design schools, horticultural colleges or by gaining practical experience in a landscape design practice.

Finding your clients

When you are established, recommendation will probably come by word of mouth, as satisfied clients recommend your service to their friends and colleagues. Initially you will need to sell yourself. How you do this will largely depend on where you operate and the type of housing in your neighbourhood, because it is likely that your first clients will be local. Advertising can be expensive, so it must be well targeted. You must also make sure that what your particular consultancy can offer stands out from other advertisers. It is often more effective to seek editorial coverage or to have a journalist write about gardens you have designed. You may even need to write the article yourself, or you may be commissioned to provide a regular feature in a newspaper or journal. Occasionally garden centres or nurseries need a designer to help their customers plan their gardens, or interior designers, builders or architects may require someone with specialist knowledge. Many clients come through social occasions with friends or acquaintance suggesting that you might like to pop round for a drink and give them a few ideas. It is, however, rarely wise to work for friends, and if you wish to be treated seriously, it is best to give your name and address, or give a card to be followed up later.

Fees

To start up your own practice you must be confident that you have enough ability and practical experience to justify charging fees for your time. Although there are a variety of possible arrangements, most designers charge on a consultancy basis of a set fee per hour or per day, to which must be added travelling time and costs such as petrol, parking, wear and tear on use of car and so on. Other chargeable expenses, such as film and developing photographs of the site, dyeline prints and photocopies, printing of reports or preparation of presentation boards, should also be added. Remember to keep all the receipts.

Your card should state who you are and what service you can offer. It should be followed by an initial consultation for which you may or may not charge, to discuss the project and how you would charge for your services. A letter summarizing the meeting should follow. This should state the scope of your work and how you intend to charge for it. A client normally prefers to have some idea of your total charges and of the building and planting costs at the outset. Showing your portfolio of previous work can help clients understand what is involved, and you may even suggest that they contact your past clients to look at your work.

Most designers work to a scale of fees, which indicates the different stages in working up a plan. It may include the following headings:

- **the initial consultation:** a visit to the client's garden for an initial consultation may or may not be charged, or may be deducted from the overall charge if you are engaged ...... ☐

- **a written report**, which is optional, but is often the basis for a garden layout plan .... ☐

- **the garden layout plan** will show proposed areas of hard landscaping, planting, paving, walls and steps, together with suggestions for enhancing the scheme with pools or statuary where applicable............□

■ **a detailed planting plan** will give the botanical names of individual plants required, together with the quantities and costs ....□

■ **the preparation of construction drawings**..□

■ **the preparation of specification documents** ....□

■ **project supervision** ....□

■ **aftercare and maintenance** ....□

You may employ a draughtsman, whose time will be charged at a lower rate, to help with some of your drawings, or you may need to call in specialist advice, such as a tree surgeon or water specialist, who may invoice the client direct. Most clients prefer to know exactly what costs are likely to be incurred before any work begins. Remember to invoice your client regularly and to follow up any non-payments.

After your client has accepted your plan, you will need to obtain quotes from reliable builders, who should be supplied with a specification, against which they will quote, of exactly what is intended. It will be your responsibility to write the specification and to pass on your recommendations on the quotes to your client.

Overheads

In setting your fees, do no overlook how much it is going to cost to run your practice. You will have overheads such as heating and lighting, and you may have other staff, such as a draughtsman and secretary, bookkeepers or accountants. Your reputation will be enhanced if you establish an organized practice at the outset, which can expand as work develops.

Executing the work

Once a client has accepted the garden layout and the planting plan, where relevant, the building work can begin. Your client should be encouraged to employ you to oversee the work, because a builder's interpretation of your plan may be different from yours. At this stage, there are three ways in which you can be paid:

■ on a percentage basis based on the cost of the work
■ on a time basis
■ by a lump sum

You will agree with the client which of these methods to adopt. The decision will depend on the proximity of the site and the type of construction involved.

If you are supervising the implementation of the work, you should check progress at the following stages.

■ **setting out** ....□

■ **excavation to remove topsoil and formation levels** ....□

■ **spreading materials already on site** ....□

■ **testing topsoil and applying herbicides** ..□

■ **ground preparation and the application of fertilizer**..................................□

■ **grass seeding or turfing**............................□

■ **hardcore base for paving** ....□

■ **laying concrete and paving** ....□

■ **excavation of tree pits**..............................□

■ **delivery and temporary storage of plants and other materials on site; checking that the correct plants have been delivered**...□

■ **placing plants for planting**.......................□

■ **watering and finishing off** ....□

The builder will normally expect payment in three stages – one-third before work begins so that he can buy the materials, one-third halfway through, and the final third on completion – and your charges can be similarly presented. In most cases you will be responsible for passing the builder's accounts for payment by the client, so it is a simple matter for you to send in your account at the same time. Terms of settlement should be 28 days.

Aftercare and maintenance

Aftercare, which is usually charged on a time basis, entails occasional site visits, perhaps twice a year for the first three years, to check how the garden and plants are becoming established and perhaps recommending bulbs, annuals or other additions. You may also be asked to arrange a maintenance contract so that the garden is properly cared for while it matures.

For most garden designers the construction and planting of each garden is the exciting culmination of weeks or months of careful planning. The new garden will take time to develop, but the client can enjoy watching it mature knowing that it has been specifically designed to enhance that particular property. A satisfied client may recommend your services to others and may even ask you to design the garden for a subsequent home. And for you, as the designer of the garden, there can be the pleasure of visiting a client's garden after several years and seeing how your expertise has helped create something beautiful and unique.

Index

*Page numbers in *italic* refer to the illustrations

abbreviations 80–1
access, 61, 74
accounts 133
acid soils 35
adhesive sheets, title blocks 63
advertising 132
aerial photographs 38, 40
aftercare 133
alkaline soils 35
annual plants 85, 88
arches 70, *70*
art grain paper 128
axonometric projections *103*, 105–7, *105–11*

bags 10
bamboos 85, 89
base plants *see* site plans
baseline measurements 28, *28*
books, reference 84, 85
borders, final drawings 64, *64*
boron, in soil 35
boundaries: final drawing 68, *68*
    introvert and extrovert
        gardens 57, *57*
    site survey 26
brick paths, 69, *69*
brickwork, symbols 81, *81*
bubble diagrams 52, *52*
budgets 25
builders 133
bulbs 85, 88

cameras 10, 12, 38
    see also photographs
card, prints mounted on 129
cards, business 132
cars, drives 61
cartridge paper 128
catalogues 84, 85
cement, symbols *81*
checklists *25*
circle templates 14, 16

clients 24–5, 132
climate 36
climbing plants 84, 107
clip boards 10
clock method, site survey 32, *32*
clothing 10, 12
colour: choosing plants 83–4
    dyelines 128
    planting plans 92
coloured pencils 14, 16, *101*, *104*, 127
companion planting 83
compasses (drawing equipment) 12, 15,
    46, *46*
compasses (magnetic) 10, 12
computer aided design (CAD) 20, *21–3*
concrete, symbols 81, *81*
construction details 76, *76–7*
contours 70, *70*, 74
copings, walls 70
copy negatives 127
copying drawings 126–9
copyright 64
corms 85
cross-hatching 80
curved designs 59, *60*
curves, measuring 32, *32*
cut and fill, 74, *74*

databases, plant 20, *20*
deciduous plants 92
decorative planting 87, *87*
detailed drawings 75, *75*
diagonal designs 59, *59*
disclaimers 64
doors, final drawing 68, *68*
drainage 26, 71
draughtsmen 133
drawing board brushes 14, 16
drawing boards 12, 14, 44, *44*
drawing equipment 12–16, *13*
drives 61
dry-transfer lettering 14, 16, 19, *19*
dyelines 20, 127–8, 129

edging, paths 61, 69
electricity 71

elevations 72–3, 80–1
  perspective drawings 114, 117
  planting plans 90, 91, *91*
enlarging drawings 128–9
enlarging scales 74
enquiries 24
equipment: drawing 12–16, *13*
  lettering 16
  surveying 10–12, *11*
erasers 10, 12, 16
erasing shields 12, 16
evergreens 83, 86, *86*, 87, 92
executing the work 133
exhibiting work 130, *130–1*
expenses 24, 132
extra-stout prints 129
extrovert gardens 57, *57*

fees 24, 132–3
felt-tip pens 12
fences 70
ferns 85, 89
finances: budgets 25
  overheads 133
  scale of fees 24, 132–3
finishing processes 129
flexi-curves 14, 16
folding drawings *128*, 129
form, plants 83, 84, *90*
formal styles 58, *58*
fountains 61, 70, *70*
freehand lettering 17, 18, *18*

geometric patterns 56, 58
graph paper 10, 12, 14, 27, 44, *44*
graphic scales 64, *64*
graphite pencils 12, 15
grasses 85, 89
gravel 68, *68*
grid system 53–4, *53–5*, 97
  perspective drawings 115–17, *115*, *116*
ground-cover plants 85, 87, 88
ground shaping 61, 70, *70*, 74
guidelines, lettering 18, *18*
gullies 71

hardcore, symbols *81*
hatching 80
headings, lettering 17
heat-sealed drawings 129, 130
height: measuring 34, *34*
  plants 85
  scale 74
  spot heights *46–7*, 61, 74
herbaceous plants 85, 87, 88, *88*, 107
horizon, perspective drawings 114–15
horizontal planes 59
houses: final drawing 68, *68*
  grid system 53, *53*
  photographing 40, *40–1*
  site plans 46
  site survey 26, 27–8, *27*, *28*, *30*
  terraces 61
human scale 59–61, 74

infill plants 85, 88
informal styles 58, *58*
information panels 64
inking drawings 126–7, *126*
introvert gardens 57, *57*, 58
inventory, site 37, *37*, 48, *49*
invoices 133
iron, in soil 35
irrigation 71
isometric projections 112, *112–13*

Jekyll, Gertrude 83

key plants 84, 86, *86*

labelling planting plans 89
lacquered tracing paper 127
landscape sections *see* section-
  elevations
lenses, cameras 38
lettering 17–19, *17*
  dry-transfer 14, 16, 19, *19*
  equipment 16
  freehand 17, 18, *18*
  stencils 14, 16, 19, *19*
  title blocks 63

levels: axonomic projections 106
  changes of 59, *60*, 61, 70, *70*, *101*
  measuring changes in 33, *33*
light: orientation 36, *36*
  planting plans 83
lighting, symbols 71
logos 62
long thin gardens 59, *59*

maintenance 133
manganese, in soil 35
manhole covers 28, 33, 71
maps 12
marble, symbols *81*
margins, lettering 18, *18*
masking tape 12
masonry, symbols *81*
mass and void 56, *56*
materials: abbreviations 80–1
  symbols 80, 81, *81*
measurements: scale drawings 44–5, 61
  site survey 26, 27, 28–34, *28–34*
metal, symbols *81*
metric scales 12, 16
microclimate 36
microfilm 129
minerals, soil types 35

names, plants 83
negatives, copy 127
nibs, sizes 66, *67*, 126, *126*
non-photo pencils 14, 16, 18
north arrows 65, *65*
notebooks 10, 12

offsets, measuring 28, *28*, 32
one-point perspective 114, 124
orientation 36, *36*
orthographic projections 105–7, *105–11*,
  112
overheads 133
overlays 51, *51*
ozalux paper 128

panoramic views, photographs 38, *38–9*,
  42

paper: dyelines 128
  graph 10, 12, 14, 27, 44, *44*
  sizes *15*, 62
  tracing 12, 14, 45, 127
parking 61
paths: final drawing *68*, 69
  measuring curved 32, *32*
  planning 61
patterns 56
  long thin gardens 59, *59*
  small gardens 58, *58*
paved areas 61, 68
paving slabs 61, *69*
payment 133
pencil sharpeners 12, 16
pencils: coloured 14, 16, *101*, *104*, 127
  graphite 10, 12, 15, 126
  lettering 18
  non-photo 14, 16, 18
pens 10, 12
  nib sizes 66, *67*, 126, *126*
  technical drawing pens 12, 14, 126
pergolas 61, 70, *70*, 75
perspective drawings 114–18, *114–22*,
  124, *124–5*
pH, soil 12, 35
photocopies 20, 128, 129
photographs: aerial 38, 40
  close-ups 40
  panoramic views, 38, *38–9*, 42
  perspective drawings from 124, *124–5*
  portfolios 129
  recording data 38–42, *38–43*
  in reports, 51
  sketching over *51*, 123, *123*
  uses 40–2, *42–3*
picture plane 114–15, *114*
plans: axonomic projections *103*, 105–7,
  105–11
  existing 10, 12
  final drawings 66–71, *67–71*
  grid system 53–4, *53–5*
  perspective drawings 114–18, *114–22*,
  124, *124–5*

planting plans 66, 82–92, *85–95*, 99, *104*, 133
  presentation of 62–5, *62–5*
  reproducing 126–9
  sections and elevations 72–81, *72–81*
  site plans 44–7, *46–7*
  site survey 26
plants: axonomic projections 107, *107*
  databases 20, *20*
  heights 59
  perspective drawings 118
  planting plans 66, 82–92, *85–95*, 99, *104*, 133
  and soil type 35
plastic, drawings
  encapsulated in 129, 130
ponds 61, 70, *70*, 77
portfolios 129, *129*
practices, establishing 132–3
presentation 126, 129–30, *130–1*
printing 127–8
protractors 12, 14

quotes, builders 133

ramps 69, *69*
razor blades 12, 16
reducing drawings 128–9
reference books 84, 85
reinforced concrete, symbols 81, *81*
reports 51, 132
reproducing drawings 126–9
retaining walls 69, *69*
rhizomes 85
rigid spring tapes 10
roof terraces 76, *100*
running measurements 28, *28*

scale: detailed drawings 75
  final drawings 63–4, *64*, 66, 71
  human 59–61, 74
  planting plans 85
  reduced or enlarged drawings 129
sections 74
scale drawings 26, 44–5, *45*, 61
scale of fees 24, 132–3

scales, metric 12, 16
scalpels 12, 16
scented plants 83
section-elevations 72–3, *72*
sections 72–4, 78–81, *80–1*
sepia film 127
set-squares 12, 14–15
shade, orientation 36, *36*
shadows: drawing shadow effects 66–7, *67*
  perspective drawings 118
  planting plans 92
shrubs: measuring 34
  planting plans 84, 86, *86*, 87
  site plans 46
site analysis 48, *50*, 51
site inventory 37, *37*, 48, 49
site plans *see* plans
site survey 26–42, *27–43*
site visits 24–5, 133
skeleton plants 84, 86, *86*
sketches *102*
sketching over photographs 123, *123*
skewers 10
slopes: cut and fill 74, *74*
  final drawings 70, *70*
  measuring 33, *33*
small gardens 58, *58*
soil; pH testing 12, 35
  samples 35, *35*
  symbols *81*
soil meters 35
spacing lettering 17
spirit levels 10, 12, 33, *33*
spot heights *46–7*, 61, 74
sprinklers 71
standpoint, perspective drawings 114–15, *114*
statues 70, *70*
stencils, lettering 14, 16, 19, *19*
steps: construction details 76, *77*
  final drawing 69, *69*
  planning 61
stonework, symbols 81, *81*
storage, drawings 127, 129
string 10, 12, 31

sun, orientation 36, *36*
suppliers 84
surveying equipment 10–12, *11*
surveys 26–42, *27–43*
symbols: final drawings 71
  planting plans 89, *90*
  sections and elevations 80–1

T-squares 12, 14
tape measures 10, 27
technical drawing pens 12, 14, 126
terraces 61, 68, *74*, 76, *100*
testing soils 35
texture, choosing plants 83, 84
theodolites 12
three-dimensional drawings 59, 105–7, *105–11*, 114–15, *114–15*
timber: decking *100*
  symbols 81, *81*
title blocks 17, 62–3, *63*, 92
tracing paper 12, 14, 45, 127
trees: axonomic projections 107
  curved designs *60*
  measuring 34, *34*
  planting plans 86, *86*, 90
  removing 51
  site plans 46, *47*
  site survey 26
  three-dimensional effects 59
trellises 75
triangulation 29, *29*, 31, *31*
trowels 10, 12
tubes, plastic 14, 16
two-point perspective 118, 124

underlining, lettering 18
urns 70, *70*, *75*

vanishing point 114, 117
vertical planes 59
views 35, 57, *57*
visiting the site 24–5, 133
visuals *96–125*, 105–24
void and mass 56, *56*

wall shrubs 84
walls: final drawing 68, *68*, 69–70, *69*, 71
  site plans 46, *47*
  symbols 81, *81*
water features 61, 70, *70*
watercolours 14, 16, *98*, 128
wide-angle lenses 38
wind, site survey 36
windows, final drawing 68, *68*
word processors 20
work places 44
writing 17

zipper tones 64
zone of visual influence 35